Heaven's Littlest Angels

Children and Miracles in Everyday Life

Heaven's Littlest Angels

Children and Miracles in Everyday Life

Kelsey Tyler

BERKLEY BOOKS, NEW YORK

This is an original Berkley Book and has never been
previously published.

HEAVEN'S LITTLEST ANGELS

A Berkley Book / published by arrangement with
the author

PRINTING HISTORY
Berkley trade paperback edition / April 1997

The Putnam Berkley World Wide Web site address is
http://www.berkley.com/berkley

ISBN: 0-425-15620-6

BERKLEY®
Berkley Books are published by The Berkley Publishing Group,
200 Madison Avenue, New York, New York 10016.
BERKLEY and the ''B'' design
are trademarks belonging to Berkley Publishing Corporation.

PRINTED IN THE UNITED STATES OF AMERICA

10 9 8 7 6 5 4 3 2

Acknowledgments

There is something very special and very private about sharing the stories of our children. We parents are protective, as we should be, of the way in which such stories are handled, the sensitivity with which they are written. Despite this, I had the privilege of writing twenty such stories, told to me by the people who hold them so dear, people who trusted me. I hope I have lived up to that trust and that this collection is as special for you as it is for me.

Because of their willingness to share, I wish to thank all who opened their hearts and bared their souls in telling what were in many cases the most precious and private stories of all, the stories of their children. God does indeed work special miracles in the lives of our children and I believe others will be touched by the stories you have shared.

Also, a heartfelt thanks to my editor, Elizabeth Beier, and her assistant, Barry Neville, for their ideas and encouragement with this and other books. You have taken a simple idea and turned it into a dream come true. At the same time, I wish to thank my agent, Arthur Pine, and his hardworking staff for encouraging me to continue this inspirational series. This is the fourth in the collection and much of what has happened in the past few years would not have been possible without you. You're the best!

Next, thanks to Angela Davis, Susan Nobles, and Sherri Reed for watching my children during several stages of the writing of this book. I never had to worry about my little ones and that is worth more than you'll ever know.

Again, I wish to thank my husband for becoming Mr. Mom during the course of deadline writing and my parents for their never-ending support. Also, Gina Hammond, Jo Ann Tumanello, Amber Santiago, Pam Hyslop, Susan Kane, and others who brought many of these miraculous stories to my attention. You have helped me more than you know.

Dedicated to:

My precious daughter:
Remember . . .
Today when I let go of your hand,
He who created the stars and the moon,
He who created your sweet, dimpled smile and
Your tender heart—
He, himself, will take hold of it.

My lovable, laughing son,
In some ways, you are nothing but a
Blue-eyed wing-dancer.
A blur of winged energy, moving across my house . . .
And my heart.
Here today, while the song still plays,
While God has loaned your musical laughter to me.
But different tomorrow, when the melody fades—
Leaving me a handful of golden oldies.
Dance little wing-dancer,
Dance across my house . . .
And my heart.
While the music of your little-boy laughter
Fills the space of right now.
The place that will one day be silent,
Without you.
Dance, my precious child . . .
Before time takes you on a winged prayer,

To another place, another dance.
Before the music grows dim and suddenly—
There stands a man.
Where once there was only a
Blue-eyed wing-dancer.
Dancing across my house . . .
And my heart.

And to God Almighty,
Who has, for now, blessed me with these.

Foreword

At that time the disciples came to Jesus and asked, "Who is the greatest in the kingdom of heaven?"

He called a little child and had him stand among them. And he said: "I tell you the truth, unless you change and become like little children, you will never enter the kingdom of heaven. . . .

"See that you do not look down on one of these little ones. For I tell you that their angels in heaven always see the face of my father. . . ."

—MATTHEW 18:1–3, 10

*T*he faith of a child is something sweet and precious, indeed. How better than through the eyes of our little ones can we appreciate a blazing sunset or a blanket of stars stretched across a desert sky? If we let them, children will teach us to marvel at the simple miracle of a butterfly and the delicious wonder of December snowflakes melting on our tongues.

Children believe with their whole being those things told them by people they love. They are our simplest and most treasured blessings. They laugh easily, smile easily, cry easily, and sleep easily. Most of all, they trust easily. Children have not lived long enough to fear deadlines, disaster, or death.

But perhaps the most endearing quality of these little ones is their absolute, untarnished faith. The faith of a child to believe without question in God and his heavenly angels is something almost universal in our world today. Not until a child grows into an adult will cynicism and doubt sometimes replace that which was once so certain.

And so we have much to learn from the children among us. We who are cynical and doubtful and we who are believing and hopeful alike can see how prayers are answered in a special way when children are involved. The prayers of children and those said for them seem to alert heaven in a way that is as certain as a child's belief.

The Bible tells of a time when people were bringing their sons and daughters to Jesus to be blessed. This angered his friends, who thought Jesus had better things to do than spend his time with children. Jesus of course corrected his shortsighted friends and declared before the entire crowd that the kingdom of Heaven belonged to little children and those who have a child's heart.

And so, sometimes, when a child is taken from this life we are comforted by those words. For what better place, what safer existence for those children than in Heaven's arms?

Ah, the lessons we learn when we take the outstretched hands of our children, when we look into innocent, trusting faces and hear the truth in their stories. When we let them lead us on a journey of faith—one which we might otherwise have grown too old and too worldly to have taken.

Let the journey begin!

Introduction

A modern folk tale has been told of a young boy, seven years old, who played baseball on his town's Little League team. The boy was not very talented athletically and he spent much of his time on the bench. Still, the boy's father, a man of deep faith, attended every game and cheered for his son whether he struck out or not.

Then one week, the boy came to the game alone.

"Coach," he said. "Can I start today? It's really important. Please?"

The coach pondered the child before him and thought of the boy's lack of coordination. He would probably strike out and swing at every ball that came his way. But then the man thought of the boy's patience and sportsmanship during the weeks he'd played but an inning or two.

"Sure," he said and shrugged, tugging on the boy's

red cap. "You can start today. Now go get warmed up."

The boy was thrilled and that afternoon he played the game of his life. He hit a home run and two singles and in the field he caught the fly ball that won the game.

The coach, of course, was stunned. He had never seen the boy play so well, and after the game he pulled him aside.

"That was a tremendous performance," he told the child. "But you've never played like that before. What was the difference today?"

The boy smiled then and the coach could see his childlike brown eyes welling up with happy tears.

"Well, Coach, my father was very sick. He was blind and last week he died." The boy swallowed hard and then continued. "Today was the first time he's seen me play."

We hear such stories and we know that this is the picture of a child's heart, a child's hope.

There is another story. This one about the captain of a ship that set sail a hundred years ago from England. The captain's family was aboard along with a dozen other people and a shipload of cargo.

Midway through the journey, on a dark and rainy night, a terrible storm overtook the ship, tossing it among the waves and sending cargo spilling about the passenger area.

"We're all going to die!" someone shouted. Panic ensued and people began running throughout the ship.

Amid the turmoil, the captain's eight-year-old daughter awoke and looked about in startled fear, her face pale and drawn.

"What's happening? Why is everyone screaming?" she asked.

"Quick!" someone shouted at her. "Get out of bed! There's a storm and we're all going to drown!"

"Is my father at the helm?" she asked quickly.

"Yes, of course."

Peace flooded the child's face and, deeply satisfied, she lay back down on her pillow, content once more to fall asleep.

This, then, is the picture of a child's faith, fresh and pure and untarnished by the things of this world.

Herein is a collection of stories about such children, whose simple prayers were unexplainably answered or upon whom a miracle was worked. These children are from cities and towns across North America. They are those we see skipping across school playgrounds and eating cotton candy at county fairs.

They are common in many ways and yet they have something all of us are longing for. They have faith, more pure and true than anything in our adult world. And because of that, they are the youngest recipients of answered prayer and miraculous encounters.

Through their eyes we can see a world where there is hope after all, where the sun dawns even after the darkest nights.

Read their stories and maybe you, too, will see the light.

Heaven's Littlest Angels

Children and Miracles
in Everyday Life

"Jesus, Please Take Care of Me!"

There was no warning on April 8, 1994, that tragedy was about to strike in the lives of Chan and Lori White. The young couple was in the middle of packing their belongings for a move from Conover, North Carolina, to nearby Hickory. For days their sons, Jordan, five, and Hunter, three, had passed the afternoons playing outside while their parents filled cardboard boxes and loaded them onto their metal trailer.

That afternoon, Lori was inside with a friend who was helping her pack.

"Daddy, can you tie my shoes?" Jordan ran down the hallway holding a pair of sneakers. "Me and Hunter are gonna play out back, okay?"

Chan swept Jordan into his arms and held him in his lap as he tied the child's shoes. "You bet," he said, tousling Jordan's straight brown hair. "Just make sure you stay in the yard."

Jordan grinned, his blue eyes twinkling, and then

he disappeared out the back door with Hunter close behind him. Chan smiled to himself and picked up a handful of mail on the kitchen counter. As he was sorting through it, he suddenly heard a loud crash, which reverberated sickeningly through the house. It sounded like the crash of a dump truck tailgate as it eliminates its load.

"Jordan! Hunter!" Chan screamed as he raced out the back door.

The three-hundred-pound steel ramp at the back of the trailer had come down onto the ground and nearby Hunter stood frozen in place, his eyes wide with shock. There was no sign of Jordan.

"Where's Jordan?" Chan shouted to Hunter, but the child remained motionless.

Chan ran toward the ramp and there, underneath, was Jordan. Blood was oozing from his nose, mouth, and ears, and the heavy ramp was resting on his head. His body was limp and showed no signs of life.

Summoning a strength he hadn't known he possessed, Chan lifted the ramp off Jordan's head and quickly swept the boy up into his arms. Blood began pouring from his sunken skull.

"Lori!" Chan screamed, his voice filled with panic.

Instantly, Lori ran to the door and stared horrified at the child in Chan's arms. Jordan was covered with so much blood that it was only by looking at his tennis shoes that she could tell which of her sons had been hurt.

"We've got to get him to the hospital," Chan said as he ran with Jordan toward their family car.

Lori left Hunter with her friend and sprinted toward the car, jumping into the driver's seat. In seconds, they were on the nearest highway racing toward Catawba Memorial Hospital.

Whenever Lori was in trouble, she would sing the same favorite hymn. Now, as she backed out of the driveway, she began anxiously singing the familiar words.

"Seek ye first the kingdom of God and his righteousness," she sang quietly, willing herself to be calm. "And all these things shall be added unto you, allelu, alleluia."

Jordan had remained unmoving and she wondered if perhaps he was already dead. Then she forced herself not to think that way. If there was one thing that characterized the White family, it was their faith. Driving as fast as she safely could, Lori prayed constantly for God's intervention and believed with all her heart that he was working in Jordan's life even at that very instant. Beside her, Chan, too, was praying for a miracle.

Suddenly, a few blocks from the hospital, Jordan coughed and began making gurgling sounds. Blood spewed from his mouth as he struggled to breathe, and as Chan spoke soothingly to him, the boy opened his eyes.

"Daddy." The boy's words were slurred and his eyes were rolled back in his head. "Sleep."

No, don't sleep, Jordan. You might never wake up, Chan thought.

Jordan moved restlessly in his father's arms, blood still causing gurgling sounds to come from his throat.

"Jordan, do you know that Mommy and Daddy love you so much, son?"

Jordan made no response.

"We will always love you, Jordan," Chan added. "And Jesus loves you, too. He will always take care of you."

The child's eyes closed once more and both Lori and Chan privately sensed they were losing him. Chan thought about the time just one week earlier when he and Lori were tucking the boys in at night. They had just finished saying their prayers. Chan explained to the boys that it was Good Friday, the day when Jesus died many years earlier.

"He died on that cross for me and you and all of us, he took the punishment for our sins so we wouldn't have to pay the price for them," Chan said gently as he gazed into the sincere eyes of Jordan and Hunter.

"I already know about that," Jordan piped in. "Our teacher

at school told us Jesus died on the cross for us and we can ask him to live in our heart."

Chan and Lori had smiled at their oldest son, nodding in unison. "That's right, Jordan."

The boy grinned. "So I did it."

"You did?" Lori asked curiously.

Jordan nodded enthusiastically. "Yes. I said a prayer and asked Jesus to live in my heart."

Now, as they rounded the corner and turned into the hospital's emergency room parking lot, Lori felt strangely comforted by the scene. Almost as if God wanted her to feel peace in the knowledge that Jordan's place in heaven was secure.

As Lori pulled up near the entrance, she glanced at her husband. There were tears in her eyes and something else that seemed like a deep serenity. "Chan, he's in the Lord's hands."

Chan nodded, blinking back his own tears. "God's in control here. All we can do is trust him."

Then Chan and Jordan disappeared into the hospital while Lori parked the car. Others in the emergency room stared in horror at the blood-covered child and his frantic father as they were ushered into an examination room. There was so much blood in his airway that he thought he was choking and he began to cry.

Chan calmed him down, and as he did, Lori joined them and took over, placing Jordan's small hand gently in hers and speaking to him softly. Again, Jordan's body went limp and his eyes closed. Around the room a handful of nurses and doctors rushed to get the boy's vital signs and insert an IV into his arm.

"How did this happen?" a doctor asked as he stood over Jordan and felt for his pulse.

Chan began to explain the situation, and as he did, Lori sobbed quietly. It was the first time she understood how Jordan had been injured. When Chan finished the story, he left the room and made a call to his parents who lived nearby.

"Jordan's been hurt very badly," he said, his voice choked with pain. "I need you to come quickly to the hospital."

When he hung up he returned to Jordan's room, closed his eyes, and resumed praying. Minutes passed and Chan was called out to the front desk to complete admission paperwork. Just as he reached the counter, the double doors opened and he saw his father standing on the other side.

Chan could read a million unspoken things in his father's eyes. Almost as if his father wanted somehow to carry Chan's hurt, the way Chan wanted to carry Jordan's.

Chan explained the situation to his father as he filled out the admission papers. When he finished, the doctor approached and said Jordan would need to be transferred to Frye Regional Medical Center across town, where they had more sophisticated equipment for severe head injuries.

Minutes later Lori called her parents and asked them to come quickly. As they left the house, the older couple telephoned a friend and asked her to put Jordan on their church's prayer chain. Before dark that evening, hundreds of people at churches in three states were praying for Jordan.

Lori, Chan, Chan's parents, and two nurses stood in with Jordan in his room as they waited for the ambulance. The boy's skin color had grown frighteningly pale and both nurses were struggling to locate his pulse.

Lori was still holding Jordan's hand and she squeezed it tightly. "Jordan, honey," she said through her tears. "No matter what happens your daddy and I love you very much and we're praying for you."

She let go of the child's hand and stepped back to make room for the nurses. At that instant, Jordan moved. Lori narrowed her eyes and Chan took a step closer to him, both wondering if the movement had been their imagination.

Then, suddenly, in an almost unnatural manner, Jordan's small shoulders rose so that he was nearly sitting straight up. His eyes were still closed and it seemed as if someone were supporting him with invisible hands behind his back. His long, black eyelashes fluttered then and his eyes opened, staring blankly.

In a weak but clear voice he said, "Jesus please take care of me . . ." Then he closed his eyes and sank back onto the hospital bed, still once again.

The nurses looked at each other and then at the Whites in disbelief.

Chan and Lori stared at their son, stunned by what had just happened. They took Jordan and Hunter to church each week and prayed with them at mealtime and before going to bed. But now Jordan was reaching out in faith at a time of crisis as if it were the most natural thing he had ever done.

Before anyone in the room could discuss Jordan's movements or his simple words, ambulance attendants rushed into the room and whisked the boy away. The rest of the evening passed in a blur.

Friends and family and members of the White family's church gathered in the waiting room at Frye Regional Medical Center while doctors performed a CAT scan on Jordan's brain. Early tests showed that he had suffered extensive damage.

"We'll let you know more information as soon as we have it," one doctor told them. "But I have to be realistic with you. His chances don't look very good."

Finally, a neurosurgeon spoke with Chan and Lori and explained the X rays of Jordan's head. The trailer ramp had fractured his skull, shattering bone fragments into the area of the brain that controls speech, hearing, and memory.

"We'll need to do surgery right away," he explained gently. "There's no telling the extent of his brain damage until we get in and see for ourselves."

He warned them that even if Jordan survived the initial trauma and surgery, he would not be the same boy he had been before.

"That ramp weighed three hundred pounds and the impact is going to leave permanent brain damage. You need to know how serious this is."

Lori collapsed in Chan's arms and sobbed. She pictured Jordan grinning from his bed the week before, talking about how he had

prayed and asked Jesus to live in his heart. He was a bright, in-
telligent child who loved to make people laugh. Now she wondered
if he would survive the night, and if he did, whether that part of
him, which she knew and loved, might be gone forever.

Then, as Lori and Chan grieved for Jordan, their friends and
family began to clasp hands and form a circle of prayer in a private
waiting area. While surgeons worked for hours in the delicate damaged portion of Jordan's brain, they prayed for God's protection.

"Please, Lord, guide the hands of the surgeons and help them
so that they can repair the damage in Jordan's head," someone
said.

"Give Chan and Lori peace, dear God, so that they can endure
this trial they are going through," said another. "And please heal
little Jordan."

The prayers continued, the people unaware of anyone else
around them but intent only on making their prayers heard. In the
midst of this, Chan and Lori felt the love of those gathered around
them and at the same time they were flooded with an overwhelming sense of peace and acceptance.

Six hours after the surgery began, the doctor appeared and
lowered his surgical mask. He motioned for Lori and Chan to follow him and then he opened a door.

"Come say hello to Jordan," he said, his eyes twinkling.

Chan and Lori moved slowly to Jordan's bedside. The child's
skin looked like parchment and his head was surrounded in bandages. Lori reached her fingers toward him and as she did a tiny
burp escaped from the boy's mouth.

"Excuse me," he whispered.

Lori felt a surge of elation. Jordan could speak, and more than
that he still had his manners. They had not lost Jordan after all.
She gripped Chan's hands in her own, happy tears clouding her
vision.

Hours later Jordan was taken up to the neuro-intensive care
unit, where he seemed to be improving with each passing minute.

"Could I have my toothbrush please?" he asked a nurse. She

stared at Jordan, then at his chart, and finally at Chan and Lori, seated nearby.

"The doctors don't know what to think about this boy," she said.

Still, despite the obvious signs of success, doctors continued to warn the Whites that Jordan could take a turn for the worse at any moment. Seizures, also, were a distinct possibility because of the severity of his head injury. Worst of all, Jordan carried a significant risk of developing a brain infection. He would have to undergo a series of painful intravenous antibiotic treatments to counteract the risk of this sometimes fatal complication.

"The medicine will be very powerful and will be administered directly into Jordan's bloodstream," the doctor warned the Whites that night. "The sessions will take thirty minutes and will be very painful for Jordan. If there was any other way, we'd take it, but there isn't it."

Chan and Lori stayed by Jordan's side through the night, holding his hand and praying for him. He looked so lost among the bandages and tubing that they began to wonder whether he would really survive. As morning drew near, Jordan moaned from nausea and suddenly the room was filled with nurses. Lori tightened her grip on Jordan's hand.

"Mommy, pray with me," he said, his voice weak.

In that instant, Lori felt her doubts dissolve. If Jordan could see clearly enough that the solution was prayer, and he only wanted his mother to join him, then she would never again wonder whether he would survive. She would take her son's lead and simply pray.

Through the next three days, whenever Jordan was awake, he asked just one thing of whichever parent was with him.

"Pray for me, Mommy," he'd say. Or, "Please, Daddy, come pray with me."

The stronger his faith was, the stronger Chan's and Lori's became.

When Jordan was moved from the intensive care unit to the

pediatric wing, Lori was approached by a therapist who had never met Jordan.

"Mrs. White," she said, "we need to make plans for your son's treatment. I've studied his chart and it's a miracle he's even alive. But now we have a lot of work to do."

Lori looked confused. "I don't understand."

The therapist checked her chart once more. "Isn't your son Jordan White, the one with the depressed skull fracture?"

"Yes, but he just got up and walked to the bathroom by himself. He's been talking nonstop all day and he's building a house of Legos on his hospital tray."

The therapist was silent for a moment. "That's incredible."

Later that day the technician who had done Jordan's initial CAT scan stopped in to see for herself whether Jordan really was showing no signs of brain damage.

She smiled as Jordan added another block to his Lego house and laughed at one of his father's jokes.

"I felt so sorry for you that night," she told Lori, her voice soft so that Jordan couldn't hear her. "I never in a million years thought you'd get your boy back like this, especially not so soon. Truthfully, I wasn't sure you'd get him back at all. I've never seen anything like it."

By the fifth day after Jordan's accident, the only reason he was still in the hospital was to receive his intravenous antibiotic treatments. The doctor had been right about them; they were harrowing and the Whites had to endure Jordan's pain along with him twice each day. The strong medication burned throughout Jordan's body for the entire thirty-minute treatment.

Typically, the nurse would come in with the medication and Lori would climb into bed beside her son, holding him close and steadying him so he could not jerk the needle from his arm.

Sometimes the boy would be sleeping when the treatment started, but the moment the medication entered his bloodstream he would wake, eyes wide with pain and fear. Then Jordan would wail aloud, begging for Lori to pray for him. And Lori would pray, as hard as she knew how. After a while, Chan could not stand to be in the room during the sessions, so gut-wrenching were the boy's cries.

The ordeal was exhausting, and one night, as the next treatment time drew near, Lori felt as if she could not possibly endure another minute of the treatment. Still, she knew that Jordan was counting on her to pray for him.

Lori stood up and walked close to Jordan's bed and saw that he was fast asleep. She pictured him awake in just a few minutes, screaming in pain, and then she sighed aloud and slowly knelt beside his bed.

"Lord," she whispered. "All I can do is trust you, like Jordan trusts you. You are more powerful than any bacteria, than any medicine, than any fear or agony. Please protect Jordan from the pain."

As Lori stood up, the door opened behind her and the nurse entered the room with the medication. Lori climbed up onto the bed and lay beside the boy, her arms wrapped around him. The nurse shifted Jordan's arm and slid the needle into his vein. He opened his eyes and started to move, but Lori patted him softly.

"It's okay," she whispered. "Mommy's here. Mommy's praying." The corners of Jordan's mouth turned up and then he closed his eyes again.

Additional nurses had entered the room, ready to help hold Jordan down once the burning and crying started. The room was still and dark and hushed as everyone waited. Drip by drip the medication entered Jordan's veins. Ten minutes passed, then twenty, but Jordan remained peacefully asleep. The nurses exchanged curious glances and waited.

Finally a full thirty minutes had gone by and the treatment was over. Jordan had not so much as stirred even once through the entire session.

"Thank you, God," Lori whispered as the nurses filed out of the room. "Thank you for knowing that I couldn't take any more."

After ten days in the hospital, Chan and Lori were able to

bring Jordan home. There were no signs of infection and he could complete his recovery in his own bedroom.

Time passed and Jordan continued to heal. A year later there was only a soft area along his skull and some hearing loss in his right ear to remind the Whites of Jordan's accident.

For a time, Jordan didn't remember anything about what happened to him that fateful afternoon. Then one day he was playing when he looked at Lori.

"Mommy, I pulled the pin out," he said simply. "That's what made the trailer ramp fall on me."

Lori stopped what she was doing and stared closely at her son.

"It really hurt," Jordan continued. "But then Jesus came."

Lori felt her heart begin to beat faster. "What did Jesus look like, honey?"

"He was just . . . all white," he said. "Then Daddy came and lifted the ramp off my head."

Lori imagined Chan lifting the three-hundred-pound ramp off tiny Jordan and she shuddered. The boy was still looking at her now, wanting to finish the story. Lori urged him to continue.

"Jesus came to see me when we got to the hospital, too." Jordan's face was serious, his eyes dim with the memory. "He lifted me up and hugged me and said, 'Jordan, you're going to be okay now.' "

Lori's mind flew back to the moment in the treatment room of the first hospital when they were waiting for the ambulance. Jordan had sat up in bed as if cradled from behind. Then, almost as if he were in a trance, he had asked Jesus to take care of him. Lori remembered her son's faith in the days that followed and suddenly tears filled her eyes.

"Oh, Jordan." She knelt beside her son, taking him in her arms. As she did, she could sense another set of arms enfolding them both, arms that had been there to hold her little boy in his hour of greatest need.

The Baby from Heaven

$\mathcal{T}$he sky over London, Ontario, was stormy gray that March 7 and the only sound in the Craenen's car was that of the wipers rhythmically clearing the windshield so John Craenen could see where he was going. Beside him, his wife, Karen, sat in silence, an occasional teardrop spilling onto her cheeks.

It was the darkest day of their lives. They had an hour before they would arrive at Victoria Hospital and Karen reflected on all that had brought them to this point.

She and John had married six years earlier and almost immediately begun trying to have a baby. But months passed and still she was not pregnant.

"We could try fertility drugs," their doctor explained. "If they don't work, we could go with a number of other options."

The Craenens agreed but believed the situation would be simple to solve. There was no history of infertility in either family and they figured the medication would allow Karen to become pregnant almost immediately.

"Thank you for the medicine, and now, Lord, please let Karen conceive a child," John and Karen would sometimes pray. "I know you can hear me, Lord, and I look forward to your answer."

But months passed and nothing happened, even after the doctor increased Karen's level of medication. After three years, the doctor tried artificial insemination but with no success. Finally, there remained only test tube fertilization, a procedure where Karen's eggs and John's sperm were harvested from their bodies and fertilized in a test tube. The embryo was then implanted in Karen's uterus.

Three times the Craenens did this but each time Karen miscarried.

About that time, Karen began complaining of sharp pain in her abdomen. The pain was occasional at first but then more constant and more severe. Finally her doctor diagnosed endometriosis, a painful condition which causes tissue to lodge in the ovaries and fallopian tubes.

"The only surefire cure is a hysterectomy," the doctor said at one of her appointments.

Karen shook her head, tears welling up in her eyes. "I want a baby, Doctor," she cried. "Not a hysterectomy."

The doctor sighed. "I understand. But endometriosis is very painful and it will only get worse with time. The chances of you getting pregnant are even slimmer than before, because of this condition. Just keep the hysterectomy in mind. It's one way to be sure you don't have to live with terrible pain all your life."

Karen left the office in tears and cried all the way home. She shared the news with John, who was crushed.

"I just don't understand," John said, shaking his head. "I've prayed about this so much; you have, too. How come God won't let us have a baby?"

Karen shrugged sadly. "I guess we'll never really understand."

In the weeks that followed, Karen dealt with the increasing

pain of her endometriosis with a quiet faith, continuing to pray about the situation and to ask God for a child. But John grew angry with God, frustrated over the length of time he'd been praying about the situation with no apparent answer.

He was at work one day when a coworker asked him about whether he and Karen were still trying to have a baby.

"Of course," he said, his voice tinged with anger. "We've wanted a baby for years."

The woman looked strangely at John. "You seem angry."

John uttered a short laugh. "Yeah, I guess you could say that."

"There's nothing to be mad about," she said gently. "Sometimes people can't have children. It's not like it's anyone's fault."

John studied the woman. "You don't understand," he said. "Karen and I have done our best to live a good, Christian life. We've asked God every day to be gracious and bring us a child. Instead, Karen's developed this endometriosis where she has sharp pain all through her abdomen."

"So you're angry at God?" John's coworker asked simply.

John hesitated. "Yes. I guess I am. I'm mad at God because he isn't answering our prayers. Why should we have to go through this when all we want is a family like anyone else?"

The girl was quiet a moment, and when she spoke, her voice was still quiet. "Why shouldn't you have to go through something painful?" she asked.

"Huh?"

"Why shouldn't you have to have this trial? Everywhere you look there are people suffering from a million different heartaches. God cares about you, still. But this isn't Heaven. You can't think you should be exempt from having a little trouble down here."

John was taken aback by her brutal honesty. Suddenly he realized he had been presumptuous with God, expecting that he and Karen would be spared from the problems that occur daily in the lives of others, even other believers.

"Well, I gotta get back to work." The woman shrugged and turned away.

"Hey, wait," John said. She turned back then and looked at John. "Thanks. I think I needed to hear that."

That night John shared the conversation with his wife.

"Maybe we should give the situation up to God and let him know that we trust him, even if you never get pregnant."

Karen sighed. "Could you really do that, John? I mean, you won't be happy without a child."

John studied his wife. "Karen, I didn't marry you so you could be a baby machine. I married you because I love you. And if we never have children, then we are still a family. Maybe it's time we get on with life and start acting like one."

In the year that followed, the Craenens began taking more trips together and enjoying each other's company. They stopped searching for new pregnancy-inducing procedures and Karen quit taking fertility drugs.

"You're not mad at God anymore, are you?" she asked one day when they were vacationing in Acapulco.

"No. I'm at peace with him. He knows I would still love to have a child, but if it never happens, then I'll always be thankful he gave me you." He kissed his wife. "And think of how much freedom we have compared to our friends who have kids."

Karen laughed. "That's true."

"No diapers, no burp rags, no baby-sitters."

Karen was laughing harder now. "Quit. Where's my husband? What did you do with him?"

John grinned. "Whatever God has planned for us is fine with me. I just want you to know I mean it."

In the next few months the pain from Karen's endometriosis grew worse than ever. Finally, she felt she had no choice but to schedule the hysterectomy.

"You could always adopt, Karen," the doctor said, empathetic to the fact that much of his patient's pain was emotional.

Karen looked at John and the couple nodded sadly. "We're not ready to talk about that yet. We still have to get through the hysterectomy."

The doctor understood. Many times women faced with an early hysterectomy needed time to grieve the loss of children they would never have. The Craenens' situation was particularly difficult since the doctor had been treating them for infertility for years and now would have to schedule a surgery that would forever end the couple's chance of having a child.

The surgery was set for March 7 and as the couple drove to the hospital that dark, stormy day they felt lower than at any point in their marriage.

"It'll be good to have you get rid of the pain," John said lamely, trying desperately to remain positive.

Karen nodded, not really listening. In her mind she was picturing children playing in their yard, a baby in her arms. Why, she wondered, couldn't she and John have a child of their own?

They arrived at the hospital on time and a surgical team was waiting. Karen was prepped for the operation and John squeezed her hand before leaving the room.

"We'll be okay," he said, as much for his benefit as hers. "God will get us through somehow."

Karen blinked back tears and nodded. "I love you."

"I love you, too. See you in a few hours."

John left for the waiting room and Karen was wheeled into surgery. They found what they expected to find—a bruised and battered uterus, ripe with scar tissue and disease. But they found something else, too.

A seven-month-old fetus, alive and kicking inside Karen's womb.

"This is impossible," one of the surgeons said, quickly stitching Karen back up. "Why didn't anyone check to see if she was pregnant?"

Karen's doctor was on staff at the hospital and he was summoned to the operating room. He explained that the medication she'd been taking for the endometriosis had also stopped her menstrual cycle.

"We've tried everything possible to get her pregnant and this past year she quit the fertility medication. I never would have guessed in a million years that she could get pregnant on her own, let alone without the help of medication and while suffering from endometriosis."

Karen was taken into a recovery room, and when the anesthesia wore off, she opened her eyes slowly and saw her doctor sitting nearby. He took her hand and smiled warmly.

"Karen I've got good news for you," he said. "You're expecting a baby."

Karen blinked hard, certain that she was still caught up in the effects of the medication. Then she looked and saw another woman in a bed near her.

"Doctor, you must have the wrong patient."

He shook his head and grinned again. "No. They went in to take out your uterus and they found a baby growing inside. You're seven months pregnant."

"And the baby's okay?" Karen began shaking and crying at the same time.

The doctor nodded. "He's fine. But we'll have to watch you real close because of the operation. There's a chance you could deliver earlier than normal."

Karen swallowed hard. "Someone get John. Please."

John was still waiting for word about the surgery when the doctor approached him. "Karen wants to see you," he said simply. "She has something to tell you."

Cancer, John thought instantly. *They got inside and found cancer in her uterus. She probably only has a few months to live.*

He stood up, feeling a heavy weight in his heart, and followed the doctor to Karen's room. She looked up as he walked through the door. Instantly he could see she'd been crying. *Dear God, give me strength,* he prayed.

"Honey, you better sit down," she said.

"No, I don't want to sit down. Just tell me what's wrong."

Karen grinned then and shook her head. "Nothing's wrong, John. We're going to have a baby. I'm seven months pregnant."

John felt the floor fall away from him and he wondered if he might faint. Then suddenly he was crying as he reached across the hospital bed and took Karen in his arms.

"It's a miracle," he cried softly. "How can it be anything else?"

The doctor had been watching the scene and he stepped forward now and crossed his arms. His face was a mask of confusion.

"I can tell you that in all my years of medical experience neither I nor anyone on staff here has ever seen anything like this," he said, pacing the room and then stopping to stare in awe at the couple.

"She has the uterus of an eighty-year-old woman because of the scarring and endometriosis. Besides that she has a severe infertility problem." He shook his head in wonder. "Now we go to remove her uterus and find a healthy seven-month-old fetus. The medical community can say what it will about this but I guarantee you it's nothing short of a miracle."

Because of her high-risk condition, Karen was ordered to stay in bed for the remainder of her pregnancy. Several weeks after the attempted hysterectomy, blond, blue-eyed Brock was born at St. Joseph's Health Centre. He weighed just under four pounds and was kept in the hospital's neonatal intensive care until he gained a pound and then was sent home.

John and Karen carried the infant carefully to their waiting car and buckled him into his car seat.

"Before we go anywhere, I have some thanking to do," John said. He smiled at Karen and then looked tenderly at little Brock as he bowed his head. "Lord, a long time ago I stopped asking why we couldn't have a baby. I accepted that we might have trouble like anyone else. But now you've given us Brock when we never expected him to come along. He's a miracle baby, straight from you, and for as long as I live I will be thankful."

Never Alone

*G*riffin Street in Salinas, California, was quiet that evening but for the rhythmic hum of a handful of washers and dryers at the Laundromat.

Salinas was a safe agricultural town and the woman did not mind using the Laundromat late at night. With a new baby and a dozen other things happening in her life, sometimes the late evening hours offered the only time to catch up on the laundry.

She hummed as she worked, folding clothes and placing them in an oversized basket, pausing every few moments to check on her infant daughter, nestled atop one of the baskets. Finally, at ten o'clock, she got to the last load of cloth diapers. She folded each one and then stood up, stretching her back as she smiled at her sleeping little girl.

She carried the basket of clean clothes carefully, with the infant sleeping peacefully on top. She set the basket gently on the backseat of her car. There was a

chill in the air and the woman realized the temperatures were probably hovering near freezing. She turned the key in the ignition and
flipped on the heater.

"Now you won't be cold," she said, her voice soothing as she
reached around and ran a finger over her daughter's tiny arm. She
needed to strap the child into her car seat but the motion of moving
her would wake her up.

Instead, she decided to run back into the Laundromat for her
last two loads of folded clothes. Then when she'd arranged them
in the front seat, she would wake the baby and buckle her safely
into her car seat.

Leaving the car running, the woman jogged the seven steps
from her car to the baskets of folded clothes waiting inside. But
just as she bent down and wrapped her arms around the heavy
loads, she heard the sound of running feet. In an instant she heard
a slamming car door and the squealing of tires across the parking
lot.

Terror streaked through the woman as she dropped the clothes
baskets and raced toward the front door. Her car was gone. She
tore across the parking lot, scanning Griffin Street for her vehicle,
but all she saw was red taillights.

"Help me!" she screamed, running furiously back toward the
Laundromat. "Someone just stole my baby. Help me! Please, someone! My baby's been kidnapped."

Arturo Garcia was at the Salinas police station for the 10 P.M.
briefing. He was a gentle man, an officer who truly loved working
with the public and doing his best to protect and serve. He had
watched while many of his peers and coworkers grew overworked
and overstressed with their jobs as police officers. And he had seen
them grow hardened and bitter to the trials on the streets.

But Garcia had a secret, something that kept him positive and
upbeat in his job, something that gave him hope regardless of the
situation. Arturo Garcia had faith.

Years earlier he had turned his life over to God and studied the biblical teachings of Jesus. He learned that he could not only have hope in all situations, he could have contentment. Best of all, he would never be alone as long as he believed that God was with him.

There were times when Garcia had been shot at, and by all logical understanding should have been hit. Instead, bullets would miss him by inches and he would thank God for the protection. Once, he faced an enormous escaped convict in a dark alley without a backup officer. As he approached the suspect, Garcia could see that the man's arms were enormous, much bigger than Garcia's. In addition, Garcia had made a crucial error by forgetting to radio in his location before confronting the suspect.

"Okay, Lord," he whispered. "Help pull me through this one."

Garcia had been able to take the man on by himself and place him under arrest.

There was a time when Garcia left the police force for a five-year stint in Vietnam. After that he tried his hand at business and was very successful.

"I just don't love it like I love police work," he told the chief of police a few years later. "Do I still have a job if I want it?"

That was 1975 and Garcia was welcomed back onto the force.

Each night since then, when Garcia arrived at work, he dedicated the shift to God, praying for safety for himself and his peers and asking God to help him make decisions that would be in the best interest of those he was being paid to serve.

That night, he was sipping coffee, listening to the sergeant give the briefing, when an officer raced into the room.

"Quick!" he shouted. "We've got a stolen car with a baby inside."

The officer spieled off the information in the report. A woman had been washing clothes at the Laundromat on Griffin Street and was almost finished when someone climbed into her car and drove away. The infant was in the backseat nestled on top of a pile of folded clothes.

At once, the officers raced from the room and headed for their patrol cars. Garcia noted as he ran that the night air was particularly cold for Salinas, just a few degrees above freezing. He started the cruiser and flipped on the heater.

"God," he whispered, "she is one of your littlest angels. Please let us find this little baby. And please don't let her be hurt."

The officers sped in different directions, hoping to trap the driver of the stolen car before he got out of the city. Garcia drove along Old Stage Road, searching desperately for a glimpse of the woman's maroon sedan. He had been an officer with the department for more than twenty years, and like so many of his co-workers, he had developed a sixth sense about certain situations. This time he was very worried.

The Laundromat was situated right next to a freeway on-ramp. The driver of the car could be fifty miles away by now and there was no way to tell which direction he might be traveling.

The infant's mother had been ushered to the station, where she awaited word about her baby. Meanwhile, other officers were checking parking lots and dark alleys. Garcia was told to search vacant lots and back-country roads.

Precious minutes passed and Garcia continued to search as he listened intently, praying that someone would find the car and the baby safely inside. The idea of losing an innocent child at the hands of a car theft was more than Garcia could imagine. He fought to remain optimistic and forced himself not to give in to discouragement.

An hour passed and then two. Still Garcia and the other officers continued their search. The time was coming when they would have to give up, but Garcia refused to become discouraged. He came to a stoplight and once again asked God to protect the baby girl, wherever she was.

It was nearly midnight when Garcia reached Chualar Canyon Road, the second area he'd been assigned to search. He pulled his cruiser over at the first turnout and stared at the grass-covered mountainside. The area glistened with frost. Quickly, Garcia flipped on his spotlights and alley lights, gazing through the night at the illuminated land before him.

He climbed out of his car and walked the area, but there was nothing but towering trees and nearly frozen branches. Garcia's breath hung in the air and he realized he was shivering.

That baby won't last long in this cold if she's been abandoned, he thought. He was nearing his car when he heard his radio crackling. Racing toward the speaker, he learned that a man they believed to be the suspect had just been picked up hitchhiking past the town of Chualar. Garcia listened intently, praying that the baby had been found. But the news was not good.

The suspect was a parolee with previous auto thefts on his record. He was not willing to give officers any additional information and he denied taking the vehicle or having knowledge of the baby.

Garcia felt a familiar frustration course through his veins. *If only he'd talk,* he thought. He drew a deep breath and considered the likely places where the man might have abandoned the stolen sedan. Perhaps he left it in Chualar or maybe he left it across town and walked to the freeway to hitch a ride. Then again, maybe . . .

Garcia sighed and started his patrol car. The possibilities were endless. He continued his search while still listening to the radio. Two hours passed and he learned that two of his fellow officers had crossed paths five times and still found nothing. It was nearly 3 A.M.

Just about that time, a bulletin came across the radio to all officers.

"Finish your assigned areas and come back in. We've done all we can do."

Garcia pulled his car over to the side of the road so that he could turn around and head back to the station.

I can't do it, God. I just can't do it, he thought. *That little girl is out here somewhere, and if we don't find her, she won't survive the night. Please, God, help me find her.*

Garcia picked up his radio and notified his sergeant.

"Listen, I have a strong hunch that the car with the baby is somewhere in Chualar. Let me look for it."

The sergeant sighed, every bit as frustrated as his officers. "We've had two men scanning that area for the past three hours. They didn't turn up a thing, Garcia. You have to come in."

"Then I'll come back when I'm off duty and check the area on my own time."

"Come on, Garcia. You gotta let it go. You've been out there all night."

Garcia thought for a moment. "How about if I take the long way back and drive through Chualar?"

He held his breath while he waited for his sergeant to make the call. "Oh, all right. But don't take long. You're the last man out."

Garcia was elated. He had one more chance to find the infant. He turned his cruiser back onto the highway and headed for Chualar.

Chualar was a small town filled with dozens of places that would have made perfect hiding places for an abandoned car. There were alleys and carports, trees and fences. A person could check the town for days and still not cover every hiding place.

Garcia turned onto a side street, his alley lights brightening up the roadway before him. Next he made a series of turns, until finally he wound up back where he had started. His heart sank. His eyes were bleary and tired and his shoulders were aching from the tension.

Only the Lord can get me through this one, he thought. "Come on, Lord," he whispered. "Lead me to her. Please hear me. I need you right now, Lord."

Instinctively, Garcia flipped his car around and headed for the first block he'd checked. His headlights lit up an empty lot that stretched toward a carport. Suddenly his lights lit up something at the edge of the parking area. Inside the carport, behind two other cars, was the top of a maroon sedan.

Garcia tore across the parking lot and jumped out of his patrol car. Carefully, he approached what appeared to be the stolen vehicle. At first it looked empty, but as Garcia drew closer, he saw the laundry basket on the backseat. The windows were open and cold air circulated through the car.

Garcia moved a fuzzy clean blanket and there was the tiny baby girl. She was sound asleep, cold but completely unaware of the danger she faced. Quickly Garcia opened the car door, and as he did, he heard the deep, measured breathing of the sleeping child.

Garcia released a heavy sigh. He closed his eyes as his hand wrapped around the infant's delicate fingers. "Thank you, Lord," he said softly. "Thank you."

Gently, so as not to wake the sleeping baby, he closed the car door and returned to the police cruiser. Grabbing the microphone, he shouted the news. "I've found her. I've got the baby."

When a backup unit arrived, Garcia carried the child to the cruiser and together the two officers took her to the hospital. As the cruiser pulled up in front of the emergency room, a woman burst through the hospital doors.

She ran toward Garcia, arms outstretched as tears slid down her cheeks.

"Thank you, thank you so much," she cried, taking her daughter in one arm and wrapping the other around Garcia. She and the baby enveloped him in a hug that lasted several seconds. At about that time the baby's eyes opened innocently. She stared at her mother and yawned peacefully.

"How can I ever thank you?" the woman continued. "You wouldn't give up. That's the only reason she's alive. She never would have survived if it hadn't been for you. It's too cold out tonight."

Garcia nodded, his heart soaring with the miracle of the evening. Then he smiled at the woman and pointed toward the sky above. "Don't thank me; thank him."

Later that night doctors discovered what Garcia already knew. The baby was perfectly fine, unharmed in the incident that could have killed her. For several minutes after the baby was released,

Garcia stayed in the emergency room playing with the child's fingers and cooing at her.

This is it, he thought, *one of those times when I know I could never do anything else but this with my life, when I know that even though I was the last man out I was never alone.*

"God was with me," he would say later. "He led me right to that little angel and helped me save her life."

FOURTH LITTLE ANGEL

"*Pray, Mama, Pray!*"

The children's choir had just finished performing that Sunday in December 1983, and Laura Sowers was looking forward to an afternoon with her youngest child, Marc. Laura's husband, Craig, had a business meeting that would take up much of the afternoon and the couple's oldest child, Cara, seven, was going to stay at church for two hours to practice for the upcoming Christmas musical.

"You and I will go have lunch by ourselves," she said, grinning at four-year-old Marc and straightening his blond hair. "It'll be our special afternoon out."

"Oh boy, Mama," Marc said and whirled around, his toy teddy bear, Fluffy, clutched tightly in one hand. "Can I have French fries?"

Laura laughed. "Of course, silly. Now, come on." She took his hand in hers and headed for the car.

Laura checked her watch as they pulled out of the church parking lot. She needed to be back at two o'clock to pick up Cara. She figured she had enough time to drive to the Broadway Southwest shopping mall in Albuquerque, New Mexico, where she and Marc could have lunch and wander through the Christmas displays.

As Laura drove, she and Marc talked about Sunday school and Christmas trees and a dozen other things that the child enjoyed. As they spoke, Laura was struck by the sincerity of the small boy's faith. He trusted God implicitly, and oftentimes when the family found itself in trouble, Marc was the first one to suggest prayer.

Laura smiled. No wonder the Bible said the kingdom of heaven belonged to the little children. They have not had time to become cynical about life, Laura thought. She glanced at Marc, who had grown quiet and was staring out the front window. It was a bright, sunny day but the temperatures were only in the mid-forties. Marc still wore his nylon jacket and the car heater hummed comfortably as they neared the mall.

"I love you, Marc," Laura said.

Marc grinned. "Love you, too, Mama."

Minutes later they arrived at the mall and made their way to the coffee shop on Broadway's third floor. Just outside the doors of the shop was the store's Christmas center, which had been newly decorated with reds, greens and silvers. Live Christmas trees hung with hundreds of lights added to the festive atmosphere.

"Table for two," Laura said, holding Marc's hand and noticing how the boy stood a little taller. He still clutched Fluffy. Marc slept with the well-worn teddy bear and took him everywhere.

"Kinda like a date, huh, Mama," he commented, hugging Fluffy tightly to his chest.

"That's right. Just you and me."

"And Fluffy," Marc added quickly.

"Yes, and Fluffy. We can't forget him."

The waitress led them to a table and they enjoyed a lunch of grilled cheese sandwiches, French fries, and root beer. They giggled about a silly book they'd read the week before and talked in hushed tones about the presents Marc was going to buy his daddy.

Midway through their meal, an older woman approached their table and smiled. Laura noticed there were tears in her eyes.

"I just wanted you to know I've been watching the two of you," she said, her eyes meeting Laura's. "And you have the sweetest relationship with your son." She paused a moment. "Hold on to that, dear. He'll only be little for such a very short time."

Laura's eyes grew dim as she thought back to the days when Marc and Cara were babies. The woman wasn't telling her anything she didn't already know. Indeed, the time when her children would be young was passing quickly and Laura was intent on making the most of it.

"Thank you," she said. "You certainly are right. They grow up all too quickly."

The woman nodded and looked once more at Marc. Then she bid them good-bye and headed out of the restaurant on her way through the mall.

Fifteen minutes later, when they had shared an ice cream sundae, scraping the bowl clean, Laura and Marc stood to leave. He tucked his small sticky hand in hers and grabbed his teddy bear with the other. Then they walked in the direction of the Christmas shop.

"Oh, Mama, it's so pretty," Marc said, his eyes wide with excitement as he looked from one tree to another.

They walked through the shop, stopping to watch a toy train circle around the base of one of the trees, and again to watch an animated Santa Claus. Finally, it was 1:20 and reluctantly the twosome headed for the escalator that would take them down two stories to the main level, where they had parked.

Marc stepped on the escalator first and Laura followed, taking the step above him so that he was riding down in front of her. Christmas music filled the air and Laura noticed how brightly decorated the store was. It made her wish for Christmas and look forward to the days of preparation that lay ahead.

Suddenly Marc screamed, breaking the peaceful moment and causing a wave of panic to rush through Laura's body.

"Mommy, help!" His voice was filled with fear and he began releasing short screams, crying for his mother to help him.

Laura had no idea what was happening but on Marc's third scream his small body suddenly jerked toward the right so that he was now facing his mother. His eyes were wide with terror.

"Mommy, help me!" he screamed again, this time louder and longer. Suddenly, Laura saw what had happened.

Marc had been wearing deck shoes with thick rubber soles that came up an inch along the sides. As the escalator headed down, Marc had allowed the toe of his foot to be pulled along the non-moving right wall of the escalator. In a matter of seconds the steel surface had grabbed Marc's shoe, sucking it down into the narrow space between the moving escalator stairs and the wall. In doing so it had turned his foot around completely so that the inside of his right foot was now against the escalator wall, buried somewhere beneath the moving stairs.

Laura bent over and saw that her son's foot had disappeared into a space that was not quite half an inch wide. All she could see was the boy's heel. Worst of all the escalator was still moving.

Instantly Laura knew that if they reached the bottom and Marc's foot was still stuck it would be torn into shreds.

She tugged fiercely on her son, hoping to dislodge the foot. But it was being sucked further into the mechanics of the escalator and again Marc screamed in pain. They were only ten steps from the bottom.

For an instant Laura froze, unsure in her panic of what to do next. She needed to stop the escalator but in that moment the task felt impossible, like trying to stop a runaway truck or a tornado.

"Please," Laura shrieked. "Someone stop the escalator!"

There was a flurry of activity at the base of the moving stairs and then, in a matter of seconds, the escalator came to a sudden stop. Most escalators have shut-off buttons located at their base and several people in the vicinity apparently knew this.

Laura released a heavy sigh. "Thank God," she whispered. They were five seconds from reaching the bottom.

Now that the machine was no longer moving, Laura lowered herself onto her knees and examined Marc's foot closely. It had been sucked so far down into the machine that everything but the very edge of Marc's heal was tangled up with the gears and mechanical parts beneath the surface.

Images of Marc going through life with only one foot flashed through Laura's mind. "Dear God," she yelled, "help us! Someone please call the fire department. Please! Call 9-1-1."

Laura looked at the place where Marc's foot should have been and knew with sinking certainty that flesh and bones could not survive this type of accident. Laura's mind was racing. Surely Marc would lose his foot. And what if he was bleeding from the area where his foot might already be missing? He could be bleeding to death and there would be nothing anyone could do for him until the firemen arrived and freed him from the machine.

"Please!" Laura screamed again. "Someone call the fire department!"

Marc was whimpering now, his face ashen. "Mama," he said. He was calmer than before but there was still fear in his voice.

"Pray, Mama, pray!"

Suddenly Laura realized that Marc was right. "That's exactly what we need to do, honey," she said. "Pray with me."

In the past, Laura had always been nervous about praying aloud. She did not seek out attention and did her best to avoid being at the center of visible events.

Now, though, with Marc's foot trapped in the escalator, Laura could think of nothing but helping her son. Even though she couldn't concentrate on exactly what to say, she prayed aloud, asking God to help them. Then she began quoting from Romans 8:28 in the Bible. "All things work for good to those who love the Lord," she said loudly. "You promised, Lord, you promised. Please work everything out here, please!"

Marc squirmed painfully and large teardrops rolled down his face. "Mommy, my bones are all broken and bleedy," he said.

In that moment, Laura wondered if she would survive the ordeal. Her vision was growing dim and she felt light-headed. *I can't faint,* she told herself. *Not now.*

"Please, God, don't let me pass out," she said aloud. "Marc needs me too much."

Her hearing began to fade and she shook her head, furiously trying to maintain consciousness. "God, please help me!" she said, her voice loud and steady. "I know you're here, Jesus, but where are you? I need real help right now!"

Laura had her arms around Marc, holding him up since his foot was trapped at such a strange angle. At that instant, soothing arms wrapped themselves around Laura's back. She glanced down and saw the shoes of an older woman dressed in polyester pants.

"Jesus is here," she cooed, speaking softly into Laura's ear. "Jesus is here. He's going to help you."

Instantly the faint feeling disappeared and Laura sat a bit straighter, still holding Marc as tears filled her eyes.

"Tell your son his foot is fine," she said. Her voice was utterly peaceful and Laura felt her body begin to relax.

"Go ahead," the woman repeated. "Tell your son his foot is fine."

Laura wondered at the wisdom of saying those words to Marc. After all, his foot was twisted into a tiny space, caught by the grinding teeth of an escalator. What reason did she have to believe that her son's foot would be fine? Laura began to voice her doubts but the woman sounded so reassuring and somehow familiar that she simply did as she was told.

"Marc, honey," she began. "Jesus is here with us. Mama prayed and he's right here. Your foot is going to be fine, honey."

Laura saw that the boy looked overheated in the jacket and she began to remove it from his shoulders.

"No," the woman said, speaking almost directly into Laura's ear. "Leave the jacket on."

Again Laura did as she was told.

"Mama, my foot hurts," Marc began crying harder. "My bones are all broken and bleedy, Mama."

"Tell him there are no broken bones," the woman whispered, her voice calm and reassuring.

Laura didn't hesitate this time. "Marc, your foot isn't broken, honey. It's going to be just fine."

"I want my daddy!" Marc cried. "Daddy! Daddy come get me!"

Laura lifted her head and shouted out Craig's business number. "Someone, please call my husband and ask him to come at once!"

Again there was a commotion as people responded to the urgency of the situation. Laura ran her hand along Marc's hair. "It's all right, honey. Daddy's coming."

Marc sniffled loudly and turned to face Laura, his blue eyes wide with pain. "I'm so glad this isn't happening to you, Mommy." He wiped at his tears with his free hand, holding Fluffy tightly in the other. "I'm sorry about my shoes."

Once more the woman whispered into Laura's ear. "Tell him you'll get him new shoes," she said.

For a moment Laura pictured shopping for shoes with a son who had only one foot. She banished the thought from her mind. "Honey, you can have new shoes when your foot's all better. Whatever kind you want."

Marc turned toward his mother once more and there was a hint of a smile. "Could I get cowboy boots like Daddy's?"

Laura nodded, praying that he would have both feet to wear them on. "Just like Daddy's," she said.

At that instant, the fire department arrived and in a flurry of motion they used crowbars to pull back the escalator wall and free Marc's foot.

Laura held her breath as the fireman removed the shredded remains of Marc's deck shoe and then the tattered sock. His foot was bruised but it wasn't bleeding. The skin had not even been broken.

"I can't believe it," the fireman uttered. He looked at Laura. "I don't want to tell you how bad I thought this was going to be."

The man's partner stepped closer and examined the foot. "I'd say that's nothing short of a miracle," he said. "You need to get him to the hospital for X rays. But I think he's going to be fine."

Laura looked up to find the woman who had comforted her during the ordeal. But all she saw was the woman's shoes and the lower part of her polyester pant legs as she rounded the corner and disappeared.

Strange, Laura thought. *She didn't even stay to see if she was right about Marc's foot being okay.*

Craig met them at the base of the escalator then and they drove to the hospital while Laura explained what happened.

"We were having such a wonderful day," she cried, tears of relief filling her eyes. "And then this happened."

Craig reached across the car and took Laura's hand. "There's nothing you could have done, honey. Don't blame yourself."

"I know. It's just that you think your child should be perfectly safe in that situation and then all of a sudden we were in the middle of an emergency."

She paused a moment. "You know, I was too frantic to pray until Marc asked me to. He was the one who knew we had to pray."

Then Laura told Craig about the mysterious woman who had comforted her and told her that Marc's foot would be fine.

"She said there were no broken bones," Laura pondered. "Then she left just before they pulled his foot out."

"Well, I'm sure she was a sweet lady but we'll have to see about the broken bones. His foot is pretty swollen."

Thirty minutes later they were sitting in the emergency room of the hospital. The doctor listened carefully to Laura's description of what happened to Marc.

"His foot isn't broken," Laura told the doctor. "I just know it isn't."

The doctor raised an eyebrow doubtfully. "We'll let the X rays be the judge of that."

In less than an hour they had the results of the X rays and the doctor grinned in disbelief. "I can't believe a person could have his foot sucked into a moving escalator and not break any bones, but you were right. The X rays are perfectly normal."

Laura pulled Marc into a hug and glanced up at her husband. "Whoever that lady was, she was right about everything she said, especially the most important thing."

"What was that?"

"She said Jesus was with us. Marc and I prayed for that and I know for sure he was there," she said. "Right when we needed him."

And a Child Shall Lead . . .

𝒯he two families had been looking forward to the camping trip all summer, and finally the big day arrived.

"Looks like great weather," Jim Hester said as the Dawson family pulled into his driveway and began loading camping gear. Jim was pastor of a Christian church in central Arizona where the Dawsons were also active members. A trip to the mountains was just what Jim felt everyone needed to gear up again for the coming fall.

"Best weather of the summer," Tom Dawson agreed.

Still, he and his wife and two young children had packed plenty of warm clothes. The campground was located in the White Mountains in northeast Arizona and the elevation was just under ten thousand feet. At that height there were bound to be occasional storms, and temperatures could drop much lower than those in the valleys.

Jim and Gina Hester motioned to their two children that it was time to go and the two families set off, following each other in a pair of vans.

Four hours later, after a stop for lunch and refueling, the Hesters and the Dawsons pulled into their campsite. The sky was clear and blue and the mountains pristine and breathtaking. Spirits were light as the families worked side by side setting up their tents.

"How 'bout a little fishing," Jim suggested. There were hoots of approval from the four children and within minutes both families were trudging along a nearby lake looking for the perfect fishing spot.

An hour later, as dusk began to fall, Jim finally tossed up his hands and grinned. "I guess we'll have to wait till tomorrow to get our fish." They had three poles between them and no one had caught a fish yet.

"Good thing we brought along real food," Tom laughed. "I can't imagine going without dinner with all this fresh air up here."

The evening was pleasant, filled with laughter and easy conversation. The children went to bed around eight o'clock and the two couples stayed up and played cards around the campfire. Clouds were building in the sky above, but the camp was in the midst of towering pine trees and the ominous sky went unnoticed. Sometime before midnight, they buried the remains of their fire and turned in to their separate tents.

The storm hit an hour later. Lightning flashed angrily across the sky and thunder cracked at almost the same instant as rain exploded onto their camp.

"Tom," his wife, Kathy, whispered. "Wake up. I think we need to find some shelter."

Tom rolled over on his cot and lifted his head. "Honey, it's just a thunderstorm. The tent's waterproof. Everything'll be fine." He set his head back down on the pillow.

Kathy wasn't convinced. The lightning and thunder were fierce, and with so many tall trees around her, she felt certain they were in danger.

"Tom," she whispered again. "You're not supposed to stay under any tall trees when there's lightning."

"So," he mumbled.

"So our tent is under twenty tall trees. We're surrounded by them."

Tom sighed. "Kathy, thunderstorms roll through these mountains nearly every night in the summer. You don't see any other campers packing up and heading for home. Now why don't you try and get some sleep?"

She rolled her eyes and sat up straighter, peering anxiously out of the flap. At that instant she heard one of the children moving restlessly on the floor of the tent. Megan's head peeked up from her insulated sleeping bag.

"Mommy," the five-year-old said, her voice sleepy, "why don't you pray about it if you're afraid?"

Kathy's eyebrows rose in irony and she stifled a grin. "Yes, honey, that's a very good idea. I'll do that right now."

Way to go, Kathy, she thought. *Nice example. You're supposed to be the one calming the kids and now Megan is the one who has to remind you to pray about your fears.*

Rather than dwell on the situation any longer, Kathy took her daughter's advice and soon was fast asleep, despite the raging storm. When they awoke in the morning, the storm had passed but the sky was gloomy gray and their campsite was drenched.

"What happened to our good weather?" Jim asked as the two families spilled from their tents, stretched, and unpacked gear so they could prepare breakfast on the cold, wet picnic table.

Kathy wrinkled her nose and stared at the sky. "I hope it clears up. Yesterday was so nice, I was looking forward to getting back to the lake."

The weather seemed to darken everyone's mood but the children's. But despite the cold clouds and light drizzling rain, the families pulled their fishing gear together and headed for a nearby stream. As they fished, the thunder and lightning returned and the rain began falling harder than before.

"Aren't the monsoons supposed to be a nighttime thing?" Tom asked. He and Kathy and their family had recently moved to Arizona from Los Angeles and he was surprised by the length of the storm.

"Yeah, they usually pass in an hour or so." Jim began packing up his fishing gear. "This one seems like it's going to be around awhile, though."

They headed back to the campground in their vans and asked the ranger about the weather.

"Report just in says steady rain all day today and through the night," the ranger said. Then he grinned. "One good thing about a storm is it keeps the bears away from the campground."

"Yeah," Kathy mumbled. "Great. I think I'd take bears and a little sunshine over this."

The Hesters and the Dawsons sat in their respective vans as the rain pounded their vehicles. When forty minutes passed and still the rain continued, both families made a dash for the Dawsons' tent, which had two separate rooms.

"Why don't we have lunch in here and then play card games?" Jim said. The others shrugged, and minutes later Kathy and Gina began making sandwiches on damp paper plates. The floor of the tent was muddy and everyone was chilled to the bone.

The rain fell for the next three hours while both families stayed in the Dawsons' tent playing cards and telling stories and trying to stay warm. Finally, Jim and Tom looked at each other and nodded.

"Honey, I think I'm going to run Jim up to the nearest station so they can check his oil," Tom said. He stuck his hand outside the tent. "The rain's let up a little. Why don't you and Gina see if you can get a fire started? We'll need one if we're ever going to dry out."

Despite occasional complaints about the weather, the children continued to play while the women began working on the fire. The men left for the nearest gas station, promising to return within the hour.

"We really need to get the fire going," Gina said. "Tonight's hot dogs over the pit. I'm not much for cold hot dogs on an afternoon like this."

Kathy nodded. "I'm beginning to wonder if I'll ever be warm again. Everything I brought is wet now and it's getting colder all the time."

The women knew they were not in danger, but the thrill of the trip had long since worn off and they worked feverishly trying to ignite the wood they'd brought.

"It isn't wet, just damp," Gina said, running her fingers along the wood. "If only we can get it to catch."

Kathy had been wadding up newspapers and stuffing them alongside the logs. Next she would use the lighter, igniting the newspaper and hoping that the burst of flames would set the wood on fire. But after an hour of working side by side, the women had only created a great deal of smoke and frustration.

The men returned then and joined in the process. Since the rain was still falling lightly onto the fire pit, there seemed to be no way to get the wood dry enough for the kindling to do any good.

"I'll get the umbrella," Jim said. "Maybe that'll help."

He found an umbrella in his van and brought it to the fire pit. There, he opened it and held it over the wood. "Now try and light it," he said.

Kathy continued to pack dry newspaper pieces in around the wood while Gina hunted for dry pine needles to add to the kindling. Tom took the lighter and began lighting every visible piece of newspaper, blowing as he worked, in hopes of getting the fire to spread to the wood.

The four of them, sometimes stumbling over one another, worked frantically on the fire until another hour passed. During that time, Luke Hester and Megan Dawson slipped out of the tent and began watching. They wore rain jackets and had pulled the hoods over their heads to stay dry.

"If we don't get this fire ignited, we can forget dinner," Gina said, wiping the sweat from her brow. Jim still stood awkwardly over the fire holding the open umbrella and advising Tom where to ignite the newspaper, while the women continued searching for kindling.

Luke and Megan glanced at each other and then at the gray skies above. Then Luke, who was a year older than Megan, motioned for her to follow him and he headed toward the woods.

"Where are you guys going?" Kathy asked, standing up long enough to see the two children walking away.

"We have to do something," Luke said. "We'll be right back."

Kathy watched them for a moment longer and nodded. "All right, but don't go too far."

"Okay, Mom, we won't." Megan smiled and then the two continued walking. Five minutes later they returned and took seats near the fire pit. They grinned at each other and kept glancing upward.

At about that time, the rain finally stopped. Jim took down the umbrella and stared at the sky. "Doesn't look like it's getting any clearer, but as long as it's stopped raining I think we can get the fire going."

Not long afterward, the fire pit was blazing and both families gathered around to warm their hands and bodies. Suddenly Kathy remembered the children's brief disappearance.

"Megan," she asked, taking a seat next to her daughter. "Why did you and Luke have to go off into the woods?"

The girl smiled sweetly. "Well, we saw how the grown-ups couldn't get the fire started and we knew we needed a fire in order to have dinner," she said. "We didn't want to starve to death."

"No," Kathy said, shaking her head seriously and waiting for Megan to continue.

"So Luke said why didn't we go into the woods and pray about the rain."

"Pray about the rain?"

"Yeah, Mommy. We went off and asked God to please stop the rain so we could build the fire. Then we could have dinner and everything would be fine."

It had happened again. First last night during the storm and now with the rain. Four adults, one of them a minister, each of them firm believers in God and the power of prayer, had worked for three hours trying to build a fire in the rain. They had used kindling and pine needles, newspaper and tree bark. They had held an umbrella over the wood and blown on dying sparks until they were left winded.

But not until their children, ages six and five, took the issue to God in prayer did anything get accomplished.

"He heard us, Mommy," Megan said matter-of-factly. "We asked God to stop the rain and when we got back here the rain stopped."

"Whatever made you think about praying, Megan, honey?" Kathy asked gently, brushing her nose against Megan's smaller one.

"You and Daddy always say if you have a problem take it to God in prayer," Megan said and shrugged. "Isn't that right?"

Kathy grinned and brushed aside her daughter's blond bangs. "It sure is, Megan. Thanks for helping me remember."

Despite the gray sky, no rain fell on the campsite until after nine o'clock that evening, when the fire was out and the families were climbing into their tents for the night.

The rain continued again through the night and let up only long enough for them to pack their camping gear and prepare for the trip back home. On the way out, they asked the ranger about the rain.

"Never let up all day yesterday," the ranger said. "Makes for a dismal camping trip, I guess."

"At least it stopped at dinnertime and stayed dry through most of the evening," Kathy said as she handed the ranger their fees for the previous night.

The ranger wrinkled his nose and looked puzzled. "No, it never let up at all. Least not round these parts."

Kathy sat back and glanced at Tom, who shrugged. "We had about five hours without rain," she said.

The ranger scratched his head and placed his hands on his hips.

"Why that's the darndest thing I've heard of. Here I was only a few hundred yards away and I didn't get a bit of relief all evening. Shoulda come over and had dinner with you all, I guess."

They finished their business and drove away, but Kathy and Tom remained silent. When they had driven ten miles, Kathy turned to her husband and sighed.

"How could he have had rain and we didn't?"

Tom shrugged again. "That happens, honey. The rain has to have a starting point somewhere."

Then she told him every detail about Megan and Luke and their prayer that the rain would stop.

Tom laughed and shook his head, thinking about how silly they must have looked as the four of them worked over the fire pit. "There we were trying everything on our own power when our kids had the right answer all along."

"So you think God heard their little prayers and stopped the rain just over our campsite?"

"Oh, I don't know, honey," Tom said and smiled. "I guess we'll never know for sure. But they saw a problem and took it to God. After that it wasn't a problem anymore. I think we can all learn something from that."

"Yeah, I guess you're right." Kathy smiled then. "Like the Bible says, a child shall lead them!"

Delivered from the Depths

There was nothing quite like a summer morning in Washington, D.C., and Marine Colonel Richard Quelette intended to take full advantage of it. As he had done many times on recent pleasant mornings, Quelette, fifty-one, donned his sweatsuit and began a vigorous jog along the Anacostia River.

Everything about the morning seemed full of promise, and Quelette easily finished his first two miles before reaching the section where the river intersected with the Eleventh Street Bridge. Then, as he continued to run, he suddenly saw a car swerving out of control and heading off the roadway toward the river.

"Help!" he shouted instinctively. "Someone stop that car!"

The beauty of that May morning was not missed by cab driver Leonard Person but his routine was a busy one and he fought his way expertly through the busy traffic. There was always congestion along the streets that led to the Eleventh Street Bridge, and as Person approached that area, he kept his eyes carefully on the flow of cars around him.

He was slowing down, trying to merge onto the bridge when he, too, saw a sedan swerving out of control. Then, before he had time to react, he watched as the car headed off the road, through the guardrail and down into the murky water below.

Lila Gamble's day had begun busier than most. She was seven months pregnant and had allowed herself to sleep a little later than usual.

"Go ahead, honey, get the extra rest," said her husband, Hayes. "But you make sure you get enough to eat. Doctor says you have to keep your blood sugar at an even level."

Lila nodded and slipped back to sleep. She was an insulin-dependent diabetic and the pregnancy had played particular havoc with her blood sugar. In addition to taking shots of insulin, Lila had to be sure to eat throughout the day. If she waited more than four hours between meals, she was to have a small snack.

"We don't want anything crazy happening to you just because you skipped a meal, Lila," her doctors had told her. "Diabetes is bad enough, but during pregnancy it's even worse."

Lila thanked everyone for their concerns but she wasn't worried. She knew her body and could tell when her blood sugar was low. She had no intention of letting herself get seriously sick. This was her second pregnancy and the first had involved the same risk. That had been eight years earlier, when was carrying little Hayes. Lila's blood sugar had been tricky throughout the nine months but in the end everything had worked out fine. She figured this time would be no different.

"It's hard to believe that in just a few months we're going to have a little girl of our own," she had confided in her husband before he left for work the night before.

Hayes smiled. He had watched Lila play with her nieces, braiding their hair and dressing them in sweet, feminine dresses. "You'll love having your very own baby doll to dress up and play with, won't you?" he said and tickled her playfully.

"You bet I will. Her name will be Courtney and she and I will be the best of friends some day."

That May morning, when Lila finally forced herself out of bed, she knew she was in a race against the clock. Hayes, her husband, had worked the previous night shift and was just having a bowl of cereal before getting to sleep. Their son, though, needed to get to school.

Padding through the house to the boy's room, Lila turned flipped his light switch. "Rise and shine, Hayes," she said, her voice cheery.

The child sat up and rubbed his eyes, squinting in the light. "Are we running late?" he asked.

"Not yet, but we will be soon. Come on." She turned toward the kitchen. "I'll get you some cereal."

She took a box from the cupboard and poured it into a bowl, then covered it with milk. "Here," she said, placing it on the table in front of her son. She stopped by the chair where her husband sat, eating and reading the morning paper. "How was work?"

"Great." Hayes smiled at his wife. "I'm beat, though. Just finish this up and then I'm gonna get a few hours sleep."

"Hayes, would you mind going with me to the florist later to pick out some flowers for Mama?" Lila asked. She enjoyed the times when she and Hayes could do their weekly errands together, and she'd been meaning to get her mother some flowers for quite some time.

"Sure, sweetie. Give me a few hours sleep and I'll be good as new."

Lila grinned and returned to the kitchen, taking the milk and cereal and putting it away.

"I'm going to get ready," she announced. "Hayes, be ready in fifteen minutes."

"Yes, Mama," the boy said.

"Wait a minute, Lila." Her husband looked concerned. "Aren't you going to eat?"

"Of course, silly. I've got to get Hayes to school on time today so I thought I'd just wait until I got back. Then I won't be so rushed."

Her husband did not look satisfied. "Aren't you supposed to eat sooner than that?"

Lila sighed. "It isn't that big of a deal whether I eat breakfast the moment I wake up or an hour later. Really, Hayes, don't worry about me."

"Well, all right. If you say so. But make sure you get right back so you can get something in your system. I don't like you messing around with that diabetes. It's a scary thing."

Hayes was especially worried because Lila was thirty-nine that year and already borderline at risk because of her age. She only had two months to go in the pregnancy and he was glad. When it was over, he wouldn't worry about her nearly as much.

Fifteen minutes later, Lila and Hayes Jr. rushed out the door for school. "I'll be back in a few minutes," Lila called as she left.

"Okay." Her husband folded up the newspaper, stood up, and stretched. "I'll be in bed. See you in a few hours."

It was 7:45 A.M. when Lila and her son left for his grade school, five miles away. By the time she had maneuvered through traffic and delivered him at the front door of the school, it was 7:57.

"Finally, you're on time," she teased. "Why are the mornings always so busy?"

Hayes shrugged and grinned at his mother. "Bye. Have a good day, Mom."

Lila leaned over, the reach awkward because of her extended abdomen. "Bye, sweetheart. I love you. Have a great day at school."

She pulled away, then steered the sedan back into traffic and headed toward home. The morning rush hour was in full swing and there was more congestion than usual as she drove up onto the Eleventh Street Bridge. It was 8:15, more than an hour since she had gotten up that morning and taken her insulin shot.

Suddenly, her sedan began to swerve uncontrollably and those around her watched in horror as the car plunged through the guardrail and flipped, dropping into the muddy river below.

Quelette was the first to react. He ran to the retaining wall near the spot where Lila's car had fallen in, looked over, and saw that the car had landed on its roof and only the tires were visible. He held his breath and jumped.

The river was only four feet deep in that area but the water was polluted and too thick to see through. Quelette swam toward the tires and felt his way down in an effort to locate the car doors. Sucking air into his lungs, he dove under and crawled through a window. Feeling around frantically, he located Lila's arm. He pulled her across the seat but was unable to get her through the window.

At about that time, he realized that Person was working alongside him.

"She's stuck in the car," Quelette shouted, coming up for air and breathing hard. Dozens of passersby had stopped to watch the drama as it unfolded. Silently, many of them prayed for whoever was in the car. Someone in the crowd called the police.

Taking turns, the two men continued to dive several times before they realized that the woman was stuck on something. Then, when more than a minute had passed, suddenly she pulled free and they were able to get her to the surface.

"She's pregnant," Quelette said. "Let's get her up onto the shore."

The men pulled her onto the riverbank. She was unconscious and didn't appear to be breathing. Quelette began working to resuscitate her and moments later paramedics arrived.

Before they loaded her into a waiting ambulance, Lila began coughing and Quelette and Person felt a rush of relief.

"She's going to be okay," Person said, reaching out and shaking Quelette's hand.

The ambulance rushed Lila to D.C. General Hospital, where doctors performed an emergency C-section.

"The baby's probably going to make it," one of the doctors said. "But the mother had a lot of dirty water in her lungs. It doesn't look good at all."

By then police had determined how to reach Lila's brother based on registration information from her vehicle. They explained the situation to Lila's nephew, who in turn contacted Hayes Sr.

"Get over to the hospital right away," he said. "Lila's been in an accident."

"Have your father get little Hayes and meet us at the hospital," Hayes Sr. said.

He hung up the phone and flew out of bed, stunned by the news. Lila had made the trip to the local elementary school hundreds of times. What had happened that she would have an accident now? Suddenly he remembered her diabetes and a sickening feeling came over him. What if she had fallen into a diabetic coma? He drove faster and in minutes was in the emergency room asking about his wife.

"She's stable, but we had to take the little girl, Mr. Gamble. The baby's in the neonatal intensive care unit."

Hayes breathed a sigh of relief but still he felt like he was taking part in a bad dream. He walked quickly toward the part of the hospital that housed intensive care newborns. When he walked in, he immediately saw his tiny daughter. She weighed just three pounds, eleven ounces and was attached to a respirator.

"Courtney," he whispered. Tears formed in his eyes and spilled onto his cheeks. "I'm so sorry you had to come so soon. Poor little girl."

He ran a single finger over her bony rib cage and another over her forehead. "Will she be okay?" he asked a nurse who was in charge.

The woman nodded. "Everything looks pretty good, Mr. Gamble. Your baby's lungs have a lot of fluid buildup but that should clear up."

She paused a moment. "A few more seconds under water and I don't think she would have had a chance." She smiled then. "It's going to take time, but I think she'll get to go home eventually."

Hayes drew a deep breath and quietly bid Courtney good-bye. Then he returned to the emergency room to ask about Lila.

"It doesn't look good," a doctor told him. "The water in the Anacostia River is very polluted and your wife's lungs are saturated with it. We're doing everything we can for her but I think you should see her as soon as possible."

Hayes followed the doctor and entered the room where Lila was hooked up to a dozen tubes and various machines. Tears filled Hayes's eyes as he approached her and gently took her hand in his.

"Sweetheart, we have our little girl. She's going to be just fine," he whispered. For a long moment he said nothing, only stroked her hand and savored the look of her beautiful face. The room was filled with the mechanical sound of the respirator as it did the job her lungs were no longer able to do.

"Lila, you always said there was a better place waiting for you, honey," he whispered. "But can't you wait and go later, when we're old and gray and the kids are grown?"

She remained unconscious, unable to open her eyes or speak to her husband.

"I'm praying for you, Lila, but in the end I know the Lord will do what's best. Remember how much I love you."

Less than an hour later, Lila Gamble died, her lungs virtually destroyed from the dirty water they had taken in. Hayes Jr. had arrived at the hospital by then and he began crying when he heard the news.

"There, there, son," Hayes said, pulling the child into his arms. "Mama isn't really gone. She's just waiting for us up in Heaven."

"But why, Daddy, why did she have to die?" the boy sobbed angrily.

"Son, God called her home. It was her time."

Hayes Jr. looked up and stared into his father's eyes. "What is Heaven like, Daddy?"

"It's a special place where Mama won't have to put up with the madness of this earth anymore. There will be no more medications for her high blood pressure and no more insulin shots for her diabetes. She'll watch over us, son. And she'll see that we're protected so that one day we can be there with her."

Hayes Jr. stopped crying and wiped his eyes. "Do we have a number or something? I mean, how do we know when our time is up?"

Hayes smiled through his own tears. "We're all going to die someday, son. We won't be on this earth forever. But only God knows when it's our time to go."

"What about my sister?" he asked tentatively. "Will she die, too."

A twinkle appeared in Hayes's eyes. "No, son, I think the Lord is going to let her live. She's a little miracle baby and God must have big plans for her life."

The following weeks were difficult for Hayes and his son, but each day Courtney grew stronger and doctors determined that she hadn't suffered any permanent damage. But Courtney wasn't the only one improving that month. Throughout Washington, D.C. a change began to come over the people who heard about Lila's car accident.

Racial tensions eased as people of all colors poured in contributions for the young father left to raise his son and newborn daughter by himself.

Others who had grown cynical over the increase in violent crimes saw the good in what Quelette and Person had done for Lila.

"For today," one person commented, "our hope in mankind is restored. Courtney Gamble will always be living proof that there still is a flicker of hope."

Newspapers shared the story with thousands of readers until

Hayes could not go to the grocery store without receiving a hug from someone who recognized him from the news reports.

"We're praying for you, Mr. Gamble," they would tell him. Or, "Please, is there anything I can do to help you, Mr. Gamble?"

Before Courtney was released from the hospital, about a month after her birth, the staff at D.C. General Hospital pulled together a community baby shower for the Gamble family. More than one hundred people gathered to give Hayes a scholarship fund for Courtney, dozens of diaper packs, baby toys, and furniture.

But the most memorable moment came when two men from the crowd approached Hayes and cooed over the tiny baby girl in his arms. Then they introduced themselves. It was Quelette and Person.

Person ran his callused fingers over Courtney's tender forearm and smiled. "You're a little miracle, sweetheart," he whispered, his eyes watery. "I hope you always remember that."

Hayes wrapped an arm around each of the men and hugged them tightly. "Thank you so much," he said, choking, his voice strained from the intensity of his emotions.

Quelette shook his head. "We wanted to save her mama so badly. We did everything we could."

Hayes stepped back and focused on Quelette. "Don't ever think you didn't do enough. You saved my little girl's life. One day I'll tell her about her mama; how happy-go-lucky she was and how much she loved the Lord. But for now, I want her to know the truth. Her life is a miracle and already God has used her to bring the hearts of people closer to him."

Rescued by an Angel

*I*t was Easter Sunday 1941, not long after the beginning of World War II, and William and Esther Porter believed they had much to be thankful for. Times were hard and most people were still trapped in the throes of the Great Depression. But William had a job in Denver that provided a home for his young family and put plenty of food on their table. They even had enough gasoline money to make the trip sixty miles north that Sunday afternoon to Greeley, Colorado, where William's parents lived.

"Sure is a beautiful day to celebrate Easter," William commented as they drove through the scenic mountain roads and eventually into Greeley.

Esther smiled and gazed out the car window. Then she turned toward the backseat and checked on Helen. The child was two-and-a-half with golden-red hair, green eyes, and fair skin. She slept as they drove and

Esther resumed her position in the front seat, allowing herself to enjoy the drive.

Not long afterward they arrived at the home of William's parents, William Sr. and Helen Porter.

"Happy Easter!" the senior Porters exclaimed as they met the young family in the driveway. "Couldn't have asked for a more beautiful day, now could we?"

"Hey, Dad, good to see you," William said, climbing out of the car and stretching. "Mmmmm. I can smell Mom's cooking from here."

The group made its way into the house and settled into the family room. Esther found a chair near the corner of the room and glanced around. For more than a year after she and William were married this had been their home. Jobs were scarce and there had been no way they could survive on their own. Especially with a newborn child. Even now, two years later, Esther was thankful that William's parents had been so generous with their home. She loved them as if they were her own parents and she was glad they lived only an hour away.

The others were deep in conversation and Esther looked across the room to where little Helen was playing with building blocks. This had been the child's first home and she was still very comfortable in it. Esther remembered bringing Helen home from the hospital and how thrilled she had been with the newness of motherhood. For the most part, Esther's memories of this house were happy ones.

But there was one memory that always sent chills down Esther's spine whenever she recalled it. Helen had been just three weeks old and she shared a room with her parents. A curtain hung across a three-eighths-inch rod, separating her crib from her parents' bed. That afternoon, the rod slipped for no apparent reason and shot down into Helen's crib, grazing her scalp and the unformed soft area of her skull.

The baby had cried fiercely and Esther and William had taken her to the hospital to be sure she hadn't suffered a serious head injury. The doctor examined the slight bruise carefully and then stood up, shaking his head in amazement.

"The rod was traveling very fast when it hit her," he said. There was awe in his voice as he continued. "If it had hit her a fraction of an inch in either direction, it would have pierced the soft spot on her head and she'd be dead right now."

Esther had clutched the tiny infant girl closer to her chest and closed her eyes, muttering a prayer of thanks.

"But she's okay?" William asked the doctor, his eyes full of concern.

"Yes. She's fine. All I can say is the good Lord must be looking out for your little one."

The doctor's statement had proven true dozens of times since then but never as dramatically as that day when the curtain rod fell into Helen's crib. She was a healthy, active child and for the most part she stayed out of trouble.

That Easter Sunday as the day wore on, Esther joined her mother-in-law in the kitchen and helped with the dinner preparations while the men talked about the war and Helen played in the house. Hours passed uneventfully and after dinner, the family wandered into the front yard to enjoy the last bit of afternoon sunshine.

The senior Porters' backyard contained a man-made fish pond that was five feet by eight feet in diameter and four feet deep. A flagstone walkway surrounded the pond, which had rounded sloping edges and contained several brightly colored oversized goldfish. The pond was a favorite for young Helen but she knew better than to play near it.

Helen did not know how to swim and for that reason the fish pond was especially dangerous. There was no way for a child Helen's age to climb out of the pond if she ever fell in. Even if she could somehow swim to the side of the pond, the wide, rounded edges would prohibit her from grasping the side and holding on until help arrived.

"You can watch the fish swim," Esther and William had

warned on a number of occasions. "But never, ever, go near the water. Understand, honey?"

Helen would nod dutifully. "Yes, Mommy and Daddy. I can't go near the water."

The rules were the same that Sunday and for the duration of the visit Helen stayed inside or on the front porch but was not allowed to play in the backyard around the fish pond.

The adults had been talking in the front yard for ten minutes when Esther began scanning the yard, checking over her shoulder toward the inside of the house. "Has anyone seen Helen?" she asked. There was concern in her voice and she stood up.

Before anyone had a chance to say anything, there was a shrill scream from the backyard. Racing toward the sound, Esther tore around the house with the others close behind her.

"Helen!" Esther screamed as she turned the corner.

The child was standing in the middle of the stone walkway dripping wet. It was obvious to Esther and each of the adults that the child had fallen into the pond.

"Oh, dear God," Esther said as she raced to her little daughter and pulled her close. Helen was crying hysterically and Esther rubbed the drenched back of her Easter dress in an attempt to calm her down.

William stood nearby, gazing down at the stone walkway.

"Esther, look at this," he said finally. "I can't believe it."

He pointed to the walkway around where Helen was standing. There were drips of water and small pools that had collected underneath her. But everywhere else the walkway was completely dry. There were no footprints or drips or trails of water leading from any point around the pond to the spot where Helen now stood.

"The sidewalk is dry, there's not a drop of water on it."

Esther glanced about and her eyebrows narrowed as she studied the walkway that circled the pond. Her husband was right. "Do you think the sun dried it up?" she asked.

William shook his head quickly. "No. It's too cold back here. The sun sets toward the west, out in front of the house. It's been shady back here for more than an hour. And Helen just got out of the water a moment ago."

They left Helen in the caring hands of her grandmother and studied the circumference of the pond more closely. "Look," William said, pointing to the pond's wide, rounded edges. "There's no way she could have grabbed that side and climbed out by herself."

Esther saw that the pond's cement sides sloped up from the bottom, making it impossible for a child Helen's size to reach the side, let alone grasp it in her small hand. Instantly, William and Esther caught each other's glance.

"Remember what the doctor said when Helen didn't get hurt by that curtain rod?" William asked, his voice nearly a whisper.

Esther nodded.

"Well, I think it's true. Whatever just happened here today was some kind of miracle. God is still looking out for our little Helen."

Throughout the evening, the Porters tried to get their daughter to discuss the incident with them.

"What happened, honey?" William would ask, getting down on his knees and staring straight into Helen's light green eyes. "Tell Mommy and Daddy how you fell into the pond and how you got out."

But each time the incident was discussed, Helen began to cry fiercely. Eventually, the couple decided not to discuss the situation. They agreed that Helen must have suffered a near-drowning and together they thanked God for his protection, asking him to continue to watch over their little girl.

Years passed and Helen grew. She had no memory of the fish pond incident but she maintained a desperate fear of water.

Eventually Helen married and moved onto the U.S. Army base where her husband was stationed. During that time she decided there was something she had to do. She contacted the chaplain on the base and told him about her fears.

"I know I could live my whole life hating the water and just do my best to avoid it," she said. "But I don't like letting this thing get the better of me. I don't want to be afraid anymore. Can you help me?"

The chaplain settled into his chair and gazed thoughtfully at the young woman seated across from him.

"When did you first become afraid?" he asked.

"I was a little girl, I guess. I don't really remember."

The chaplain nodded. "Did you ever have an accident involving water?"

Helen thought back. Then she remembered. "Yes! Actually, I don't know if it was an accident or what it was. I was nearly three years old and I couldn't swim and my parents say I fell into my grandparents' fish pond. I don't remember any of the details."

A knowing look came across the chaplain's face. "Helen," he said, "I believe if we could help you remember what happened back when you were a little girl, we could understand the problem you have with water."

Over a series of counseling appointments, the chaplain helped Helen drift back through her memory to the day when she had been two-and-a-half and had visited her grandparents' house that Easter Sunday.

Eventually, she was able to describe the scene.

"I was in the backyard," she said, her eyes glazed over from concentration. "I can see it. There was a big fish pond in the middle of the yard and I walked toward it. Inside were the biggest goldfish I'd ever seen. I wasn't supposed to touch them. Mommy and Daddy both told me not to touch them. But I wanted so badly to see how they felt, to pet them just once.

"So I leaned over and then all of a sudden I fell into the water."

Helen screamed and covered her eyes, the memory vividly real.

"It's okay, Helen," the chaplain said calmly. "What happened next?"

"I couldn't get out; I was thrashing about and swallowing water. My head was under and no one could hear my screams. I was drowning."

Suddenly Helen gasped. "That's what happened! I remember everything now."

The chaplain leaned forward in his chair. "Go on, Helen. What happened then?"

"I was sinking and my arms and legs weren't trying to fight the water anymore. Then suddenly there was a man there above me dressed all in white. He reached into the water and put his hands under my arms. Then he lifted me up and set me down on the walkway."

"Where did he go then?" the chaplain asked, confused by the young woman's story. Where had the man come from and why was he dressed completely in white?

Helen paused a moment, searching the long-ago scene that was unfolding before her eyes. "He disappeared. He just set me down and disappeared."

Helen's eyes came back into focus and she stared at the chaplain. "That's impossible, isn't it, Pastor?"

"What does your father say about the event?"

"Well, he says they were in the front yard of my grandparents' house and heard me screaming. They ran to me and I was standing in the middle of the walkway dripping wet. They never knew how I got there or how I'd fallen in."

"Was there anything else?"

Helen thought a moment, then she remembered. "Yes! My parents both remember that there were no wet footprints leading from the pond to where I was standing when they found me. There was no water anywhere on the walkway except right underneath me." Helen thought a moment.

"But there must have been some footprints," she continued. "Otherwise how did that man in white get me from the pond to the place where he put me down? You don't think . . . ?"

The chaplain smiled kindly and settled back into his chair once more. "I'm not sure I can explain it fully, Helen, but I do know this. The Bible says God protects us with guardian angels. Your rescuer was dressed all in white and left no footprints on the walk-way.

"We'll never know exactly who he was, but in my opinion God saved your life that afternoon. And a certain guardian angel returned to heaven with wings wet from the water of a goldfish pond in Greeley, Colorado."

The Blond, Blue-Eyed Miracle Baby

*W*hen Jessica Root became pregnant with her third child, she and her husband allowed themselves to dream. They had been blessed with two healthy sons, Teddy, five, and Wesley, who had just had his first birthday. The boys were happy children and both had the dark eyes and dark hair of their parents.

"You know what I wish," Andy Root said one evening as he and Jessica rested on the living room sofa.

"What?"

Andy placed his hand on his wife's abdomen. "I wish we could have a blond, blue-eyed little girl. Wouldn't that be something?"

Jessica uttered a short laugh. She had dark hair and her husband's hair was even darker. Both their boys had Andy's deep brown eyes as well. There were no blond, blue-eyed people in either of their families. "Good luck," she said, grinning.

"I know, I know," Andy said and pulled Jessica closer. "Just dreaming, I guess."

The first three months of Jessica's pregnancy passed by normally. She was busy at home with the boys and Andy continued his work as a special education teacher in Windsor, Ontario, a busy Canadian city just north of Detroit, Michigan.

Andy's students were mentally retarded and each held a special place in his heart. Oftentimes he would come home and play with his sons, silently thanking God for their strong and healthy minds. On more than one occasion he had discussed his students with Jessica and pondered how they would deal with such a child themselves.

"It would be so hard to see one of my own children go through what my students go through," Andy would say. "But I know I would love that child the same as any other."

Jessica would agree and they would put the matter out of their minds.

When Jessica was four months pregnant, her doctor ordered a routine ultrasound to make sure the baby was developing normally. After the test, Jessica's doctor ushered her into his office and closed the door. He looked at a report on his desk and cleared his throat.

"It seems we have a problem," he said. "Something has shown up on the ultrasound and I'd like you to see a specialist."

"It sounds serious." Jessica shifted uneasily in her chair and searched the doctor's face for information.

He nodded solemnly. "I won't lie to you, Jessica. It is serious. There's something developing at the base of the baby's neck and it looks like cystic hygroma, a rare condition involving fluid buildup in the lymph system."

"What does that mean for the baby?"

He handed her the name and phone number of a specialist in London, ninety miles north of Windsor. "Get an appointment with him and see what he says about it. Then we'll go from there."

A week later, Jessica and Andy drove to London, where technicians performed another, more sophisticated ultrasound on the unborn child. The diagnosis was the same.

"She has cystic hygroma, which is a rare—"

"She?" Andy interrupted.

The doctor glanced at his notes once more. "Uh, yes. It's a girl."

The couple remained silent but Andy squeezed Jessica's hand tightly.

"What I was saying is that this is a very rare condition and almost always life-threatening for the baby."

He went on to say that the baby's lymph system was not re-distributing fluids throughout her body. Instead it was gathering at the base of the skull and developing into fluid sacs that would eventually circle her neck like so many sections of an orange and choke her to death.

"Can you tell how serious her condition is compared to others you've seen?" Jessica asked. Tears spilled from her eyes and slid down her cheeks.

"It's very serious. I wouldn't usually see this much fluid buildup until the thirtieth week. I'm afraid she won't live more than a couple months at most."

"Isn't there anything you can do for her? Surgery in the womb, something?" Andy was devastated. Jessica was carrying their tiny daughter and now she was being given a death sentence before she even had a chance to live.

The doctor shook his head sadly. "No, I'm sorry. The only thing I can suggest is to terminate the pregnancy and try getting pregnant again in a few months."

Jessica's eyes grew wide. "You mean abort the baby?"

The doctor nodded. "Mrs. Root, your baby will die anyway. It'll be much easier if you go ahead and terminate now. This is the standard recommendation for cystic hygroma. If you carry until the fetus dies, you'll have a long, difficult labor. Fluid will have to be removed from each of the sacs around her neck before she will come through the birth canal. It would be far more traumatic to deliver a dead baby than to terminate the pregnancy now, while the fetus is so small."

Jessica sat up straighter in her chair. "Doctor, you should know something about us." She stared into her husband's eyes and saw his love and concern. "We won't abort this baby. If she doesn't survive the pregnancy, then we'll deal with that situation when it comes. But my little girl won't die at my hands. I won't do it."

The doctor sighed and set his elbows on his desk. "We don't agree with terminating pregnancies, either, Mrs. Root. This is a Catholic hospital and it is not our policy to do abortions. However, in this situation, there is absolutely no reason to continue the pregnancy."

"Tell me this," Jessica said. "If I continue the pregnancy, will I be in any danger?"

"No, none at all."

"Then I want to continue it. There will be no termination."

The doctor paused a moment, understanding the couple's dilemma. "You must understand that your child has a fatal condition. Continuing the pregnancy will only prolong the suffering of you and your family."

Andy spoke up then. "You mean, she has no chance of surviving. None at all?"

Again the doctor sighed. "If by some very slim chance she survived the pregnancy, your wife would have to go through a very long labor where we would be suctioning fluid from the sacs around your daughter's neck. Then as soon as she was born, if she survived the delivery, she would be rushed into surgery so the sacs could be removed and so we could operate on any other organs that might be drowning in fluid. Then, if she still survived, she would be mentally retarded. This is a condition that often goes along with cystic hygroma in female babies."

"Well then that's the chance we'll take." Jessica stood up and smiled at the doctor through eyes glazed with tears. "Sometimes you just have to trust God on these matters, Doctor."

They made an appointment for the following month and returned to their car. The drive home was one of the longest in their lives.

"Why us, Andy?" Jessica cried. She felt defeated and exhausted and completely brokenhearted for the tiny child she was carrying.

Andy reached over and held her hand in his. "God has a plan in all this, Jessica. We need to pray and have everyone we know pray. God can heal her, honey. You know that."

Jessica nodded but the tears continued to stream down her face. "I know. But the ultrasound doesn't lie, Andy. She has this, this thing growing on her neck and it's going to choke her to death." She was sobbing now and she buried her head in her hands. "I feel so helpless. Her little body is trying to grow and develop and all the while she's being slowly strangled. And there's nothing we can do to help her."

Andy's eyes filled with tears and for a while they were both silent, lost in their shared grief. Finally, when they were a few minutes from Windsor, Jessica took a deep breath and slowly released it.

"It's the saddest I've ever felt about anything," she said softly. "But you're right. We need to trust God that he has a plan of some kind. At least then he will give us the strength we need to be able to handle the next five months."

They told Teddy about the baby's problem that night before bedtime.

"The baby in Mommy's tummy is a little girl," Andy explained gently. Jessica sat near him, quietly wiping the tears from her cheeks. "But she is very, very sick, Teddy."

The five-year-old child nodded his understanding. "Like when I had the flu?"

Andy smiled sadly. "Yes. Only much worse. The doctors said that she might die before she's born."

The child's eyes grew wide in concern. Andy continued.

"But we decided we'd ask Jesus to help us and whatever happens we know that he will be there."

After that, every night the couple would pray with young

Teddy in his room and the child would add his prayers for his sister.

"Dear God, please make my sister to be fine," he would say. "Please don't let her die."

Sunday came and after the service Andy and Jessica went in front of their Christian church family and asked for prayers.

"It seems there's a very serious problem with our unborn little girl," Andy said, his voice cracking. He pulled Jessica closer to him and blinked back tears. "The doctors think she'll die before she's born and that Jessica should have an abortion." He swallowed the lump that was forming in his throat. Jessica smiled at him through watery eyes and continued for him.

"We told the doctors that if the baby dies we'll deal with that. But she won't die at our hands. It'll have to be God's decision."

A sob escaped and a flood of tears spilled from her eyes. "Please pray for us. Pray that we will have strength to handle what God has in store for us."

Throughout the congregation people were crying unashamedly, their hearts reaching out to Andy and Jessica for their uncertain future.

The praying began immediately. That afternoon a group of grandmothers at the church made the Roots' unborn baby their top prayer concern. They contacted other women they knew at other churches in the Windsor area and the prayer chain grew.

In addition, Andy's parents and Jessica's parents prayed constantly for God to work a miracle and heal the tiny girl so she could survive the pregnancy.

Over the next few days, the despair that gripped Andy and Jessica and even their five-year-old son, Teddy, began to dissipate. They were not sure what God would do but they trusted him and believed he would help them handle whatever came their way.

Six weeks passed and Jessica and Andy returned to London for another appointment with the specialist. This time the atmosphere during the ride up was completely different. The couple was calm and strangely peaceful. Andy shared anecdotes about the students he worked with and silently the couple knew that one day the anecdotes might be about their own daughter. If she lived that long.

Jessica was scheduled to meet with the doctor first and then have an ultrasound done. When he was finished examining her, Jessica sat up and looked intently at him.

"You didn't tell us the odds," she said quietly. "What are the odds that this baby will survive?"

The doctor leaned against the wall and folded his arms. "There is less than a one percent chance that this child will survive the entire pregnancy. If she does, there is maybe a fifty percent chance that she will survive the delivery and the surgery involved to remove the fluid around her neck. The odds get worse from that point on."

Jessica could feel the blood drain from her face. The peace she had been feeling vanished and again she was gripped with sorrow as she considered the child inside her.

The doctor saw her reaction and responded in a gentle voice. "There is still time to terminate the pregnancy, Mrs. Root. But it has to be your decision. I could have it scheduled right away. This afternoon."

Jessica looked at her husband and shook her head quickly. "No. Her chance may be almost nothing but I can't take that chance away from her."

The couple left the office and headed toward the room where sonograms were performed. Andy waited in the hallway while a technician turned down the lights and began scanning Jessica's abdomen. Images appeared on the screen and Jessica wished she could tell what she was looking at.

Minutes passed and Jessica began to wonder why the test was taking so long. She moved, trying to get comfortable, and the technician looked at her curiously.

"Do you know why you're in here? Why you're having this ultrasound?"

Terror streaked through Jessica's body. *There's something worse,* she thought. *They've found something worse.*

"Well," she began, her voice unsteady, "the baby has cystic hygroma and apparently there's a lot of fluid building up around her neck in a series of sacs."

The technician nodded absently. "All right, I'm going to take these pictures up to my supervisor and we'll check them over. Stay here until I get back, just in case I need to continue the examination."

Jessica nodded and watched the woman leave. Alone in the dark room, she let her eyes wander to the machine that held the captured image of her unborn child. There were dark areas and fuzzy white areas and assorted lines. But there was no way for her untrained eyes to understand what she was seeing. She felt tears stinging again and she wondered what else could have gone so wrong that the technician would want to take the pictures to her supervisor.

Silently she began to pray, repeating scriptures that promised hope and peace and telling herself everything would be all right. Even if it didn't feel that way.

Ten minutes later the technician returned.

"Okay, you can get up," she said pleasantly. "We won't need any more pictures today. Your doctor wants to see you in his office as soon as you can get there."

Jessica studied the woman. If the news was worse than before, the technician certainly was hiding it well. For a split second, Jessica allowed herself to hope. Perhaps the news wasn't bad. Maybe the news was actually good. Maybe the fluid sacs had stopped growing.

She explained what was happening to Andy as they walked down the hallway and rode the elevator to the doctor's office. After they were seated, he strode into the room smiling, his face beaming.

"I have good news," he said, his words tumbling out in excitement. "Something has happened that I have never seen or heard of in my years as a doctor. The fluid sacs have regressed and disappeared almost completely. The fluid is being redistributed throughout her body in a normal manner so that the sacs are nearly empty. Your baby will definitely live through the pregnancy."

Jessica released a cry and collapsed in Andy's arms, happy tears filling her eyes.

"Thank God," Andy muttered as he held his wife and grinned at the doctor.

"There is no medical explanation for what has happened here. I thought you should know that."

Andy smoothed his hand over Jessica's hair and smiled. "Doctor, we've had hundreds of people praying from this little girl. Everyone from a group of grandmothers to our five-year-old son. What has happened is a miracle."

The doctor shrugged. "Well, we can't really define it that way medically. We can only document her case and state that there is no medical explanation. Those things happen."

His expression grew more serious. "There is one problem," the doctor interrupted. "She will probably still have Turner's Syndrome as a result of the damage that was done when the sacs were filled with fluid and she will still have to have surgery when she's born. In other words, she will most likely still have mental retardation."

Jessica pulled away from Andy and smiled as she shook her head. "No, Doctor. God doesn't do half a miracle. The baby will be born fine."

"Don't get your hopes up," he said. "The damage has already been done, even if the fluid has somehow regressed from the sacs."

The doctor suggested that Jessica have amniocentesis done to determine information about the baby's chromosomes.

"Then we'll know for sure what we're dealing with," he said.

"There's a risk of miscarriage with that procedure," Jessica said calmly. "Would there be something that could be done to help the baby if the condition is found?"

The doctor shook his head. "No, it would just help you prepare."

Again Jessica smiled. "We'll prepare by praying about it, Doctor. I don't want the test done."

"Okay, but do this for me. When the baby's born, have her tested and make sure the results are sent to my office."

When they left the hospital that day, Andy squeezed Jessica's hand and grinned. "God heard our prayers. He's going to let me have my little blond, blue-eyed angel after all."

"Honey," Jessica teased, her voice filled with mock warning. "Don't get yourself worked up about a blond, blue-eyed girl. Look in the mirror and ask yourself if your daughter could have anything but your beautiful dark hair and dark eyes."

"Never mind," Andy said, teasing in return. "You can be a doubter but I know she's going to be a blond, blue-eyed little angel."

Weeks passed and then months. At the end of Jessica's eighth month of pregnancy, another ultrasound was performed and this time the results were perfect.

"There is no difference between your ultrasound and that of a perfectly normal pregnancy," she was told. "Surgery will not be necessary."

Jessica and Andy were not surprised. The prayers continued.

Finally, one morning, a week before Jessica's due date, she went into labor. Although the baby seemed normal on the ultrasound tests, Jessica had been warned that she would probably still have a long, arduous labor. Instead, Robin was born June 8, 1990, at 8:01 A.M.—just forty minutes after arriving at the hospital. Tests were done immediately and her physical examination proved her to be completely healthy.

Two weeks later the blood work came back. Robin's chromosomes were completely normal. When the doctor received the results, he held one final meeting with the couple.

He played with Robin's tiny fingers and tickled her under her chin. Then he turned to Andy and Jessica.

"I want you to know," he said, his eyes misty, "Robin has changed the way I'll advise patients with this disorder in the future.

If you'd followed my advice . . ." His voice trailed off. "I just thank God you didn't."

As Robin grew, the only sign that remained of her ordeal in the womb was a slight thickening at the base of her neck where the sacs had once grown, filled with fluid that could have choked her to death.

Once, when Robin was five, Jessica was doing up the buttons of the little girl's blouse and she found herself struggling with the top button. She smiled then and studied Robin's face.

"You'll always have a hard time with those top bottons because your neck is a little thicker than some," she said. "That's God's way of reminding you that you were a miracle."

Robin nodded in earnest, her blond ponytail bobbing and her blue eyes filled with awe.

"God looked after me when I was in your tummy, Mommy," she said. "Daddy says I'm his miracle baby."

Jessica pulled her daughter tight and smiled through her tears. "Yes, honey. You're our little blond, blue-eyed miracle baby."

Marty's Miracle Gift Exchange

*D*iane Rayner always cherished the wonder of Christmas and the magical feelings of joy that went with the holiday season. She pondered frequently the first Christmas two thousand years ago, when on a clear night a new and brilliant star shining over Bethlehem announced the miracle of God's son coming to earth as a child. It seemed that no matter how crimped the family budget was the Christmas holidays were always rich in spirit for the Rayners.

Especially that Christmas when Diane's youngest child, Marty, was eight years old.

Marty was a blond, brown-eyed boy whose smile could light a room. Because of a prolonged illness years earlier, he was deaf in his left ear and had a habit of cocking his head to one side so he could hear better when someone spoke to him. It was a deafness doctors claimed they were unable to repair.

That year, Diane and her children had just moved

into a mobile home in a forested area outside Redmond, Washington. The typical rainy winter season seemed never to let up. Dark gray skies perpetually pounded the muddy ground with a chilling downpour.

But inside the small trailer, the Rayners shared a gleeful anticipation as Christmas neared. Still, no one was happier than Marty. He had a new best friend named Kenny and for the past few months the two boys had been inseparable. The rainy northwest weather was never a deterrent for the young boys.

Their world of adventure was in the wooded horse pasture bordering both their homes. The pasture also had a beautiful meadow with a stream running through it, a magnificent playground, a dream come true for the adventurous twosome.

They would play for hours in the woods and meadow, searching for frogs and grass snakes along the stream. Sometimes they would dangle carrots for the horses or hang suet balls coated with seeds for the birds. Once in a while they would offer a spoonful of peanut butter to a perplexed squirrel. Other times they would remodel their scrap-wood fort, searching forgotten treasure and acting out a multitude of imaginary scenarios.

The pasture that bordered their homes was protected by an electric fence, and shortly after Marty moved in, both boys became adept at slithering under the lowest hot wire to avoid what could be a serious electrical shock.

As Christmas drew closer, Diane realized that Marty was acting secretive, hiding away the few pennies he earned for allowance and taking special care to make his bed and take out the trash. He even helped his older siblings set the table at night so they were ready to eat dinner as soon as their mom got home from work.

"What are you up to, anyway?" Diane would ask, sweeping the boy into a hug.

Marty would shrug, his big brown eyes dancing with excitement. "It's a Christmas surprise, Mom." And then he would hurry off to complete another chore.

Pinching pennies was sometimes quite a challenge for this family of four, but Diane, a working single parent, taught her children to be creative, using their imagination and inexpensive household items to decorate their home for Christmas. There were woven paper ornaments on the tree and handmade gifts underneath. Diane tried to make her children feel as if they had been blessed with abundance. In her words, the Lord had provided them with elegance on a shoestring.

Many times Kenny joined in the cookie baking, craft projects, and decorating, working alongside the Rayners at their small kitchen table. But then the boys would have an idea and instantly they would be out the door, sliding cautiously under the electric fence and playing once more in the fields. Then, in an hour or so they would be back at Diane's table, helping make paper creations or stringing popcorn for the tree.

"Remember," Diane would tell her children on those cold, rainy afternoons. "Christmas is a celebration of the Christ child's birthday. It isn't about receiving a lot of toys and gifts for yourself. It's about giving treasure, gifts of love, to others. That's what God did when he sent his baby son to us that very first Christmas."

Diane was jubilant at the thought of Marty's special gift. Her youngest child seemed to understand the Christmas message better than anyone and as December wore on he worked and saved like never before.

As financially difficult as things were for the Rayners, Diane knew that Kenny's family was struggling even harder to make ends meet.

Even little Marty could see how Kenny's family scrimped to survive month to month on their meager income. As Christmas neared, Diane suspected her son was saving his money to buy something extra special for Kenny's Christmas.

Less than a week before Christmas, Diane was making Danish cinnamon cookies one night when Marty approached her, his eyes filled with pride.

"Mom, I bought Kenny a Christmas present," he said, bursting with excitement. "Wanna see it?"

Diane pulled her hands out of the dough she'd been kneading and washed them in the sink. "Of course I do," she said. Then she dried her hands carefully on a towel. "Let's see what you have there, little guy."

Marty smiled and his enthusiasm was contagious. "Well, it's something he's wanted for a long time, Mom," the boy said.

He carefully pulled a small box from his pocket and lifted the lid. Diane peered inside and saw a small plastic pocket compass; the treasure Marty had spent weeks saving for.

"It's a wonderful Christmas gift," Diane said and she smiled at Marty. But even as she did, her heart filled with doubts. Kenny's mother was an admirable and fiercely proud lady, and though they were barely surviving, she would refuse any offer of charity. It was doubtful that Kenny's family could afford to exchange gifts among themselves, and Diane knew there was no way they could purchase presents for people outside the family.

Diane realized she had to explain the situation to Marty. She told him that although his gift would come with the best intentions, Kenny's mother might not let him accept it.

Marty grinned. "I know, Mom," he said. "But it's going to be a secret. They'll never, ever know who it's from. It'll stay a mystery."

Diane studied the child before her and smiled with pride. Not only had he saved his allowance and purchased a gift for his friend, he had already devised a way to make it a secret so Kenny's family wouldn't feel awkward.

This is truly the spirit of giving, Diane thought. *This is what Christmas is all about.*

Christmas Eve finally arrived along with cold, continuous rain and dreary gray skies. Inside the Rayners' small trailer home Diane and her three children bustled about making sure every gift was wrapped perfectly and carefully placed under the tree. Friends and family were planning to drop by the next day to celebrate the Christ child's birthday and Diane busied herself with final preparations.

As darkness fell over the Pacific Northwest, Diane worked in her kitchen and stared out the window at the dismal rain. Somehow it didn't seem right that Christmas Eve would have the same gloomy bone-chilling rain as any other winter night.

Where is the mystery, the magic, the miracle, God? she wondered silently.

Because of the heavy cloud cover there wasn't a single star in the sky and Diane wondered how anything strange and wonderful could happen on such a miserable night. Certainly this soggy evening could not compare with the clear and star-filled night when a miracle happened and the Christ child came to earth many centuries ago.

Diane sighed and crossed the tiny kitchen to check on the ham and bread in the oven. As she did, she saw Marty walk quietly toward the coat closet and slip his coat over his flannel pajamas. In his hand he clutched the small, brightly wrapped gift for Kenny.

"Be right back, Mom," he whispered. The little boy sounded so serious, about to undertake his secret mission. But there was a twinkle in his eyes that lifted Diane's spirits. Just how proud could a mother be? she wondered.

"Be very, very careful." She wiped her hands on her apron and watched her son disappear through the front door.

Through the rain-drenched wooded pasture Marty ran, traveling as quickly as his short little legs would carry him. He slid carefully under the electric fence and sped all the way to Kenny's house. Quietly he moved up the steps, placing the gift just inside the screen door. His heart raced with anticipation as he rang the doorbell.

Then in a flash, Marty flew down the steps and back into the rainy, dark night, running as fast he could. He had to get away so that Kenny's family wouldn't see him.

But in his hasty exit he forgot about the electric fence.

Without warning, Marty suddenly crashed against it and was immediately thrown onto the wet ground, his small body reeling from the painful electric shock. For several minutes Marty lay on the ground, tingling and trying to catch his breath.

Then he forced himself to his feet, felt his left cheek and winced. The hot wire had snagged him under his ear and that side of his face was burning with pain.

He was unsteady as he made his way back to the trailer. Rain soaked through his coat into his pajamas and he was drenched by the time he stumbled inside. Diane gasped when she saw him and rushed to his side.

"Marty, what happened to you?" she knelt beside him, wrapping her arms around his muddy body.

"The fence," Marty cried. "I forgot about the electric fence."

Diane felt sick. She pictured her generous little son jolted to the ground in the moments after delivering such a special gift. She could see that Marty was still dazed from the shock and she carefully examined the burn mark, a red line developing along the left side of his face from his mouth to his ear.

After tending the burn, Diane drew him a warm, soothing bath, made him a hot cup of cocoa, and within a short time, wearing fresh, dry pajamas, he was feeling much better. Just before Diane tucked him into bed, Marty remembered Kenny's gift.

"Know what?" he whispered.

"What?" Diane reached for the boy's hand and held it gently in her own. She was disappointed that the boy's gift-giving had turned into such a painful event. Especially on Christmas Eve.

Marty smiled then and Diane could see he'd forgotten about the burn. "He didn't see who delivered the gift, Mom. I'm sure he doesn't know it's from me."

Diane smiled sadly. "You are a very special and kind person, Marty. Your mom is extremely proud of you."

But hours later, Diane was still depressed about the incident. Marty had saved for months for that gift and had taken it to Kenny with all the love a young boy could muster. In return he was badly shocked, thrown to the muddy, wet ground, and his face was branded with a sore, ugly red burn blister.

Diane wrestled with her thoughts. *He was doing what you want, Lord,* she prayed silently. *But what happened tonight makes this Christmas Eve far worse than any night we've had all year. No wonderful miracles or mysterious awesome wonders. Just misery for a little boy. It doesn't seem fair, Lord.*

The next morning, Christmas Day dawned sunny and warm. The rain had finally stopped, and after days of cold, gloomy weather, sunshine filled the skies. The children awoke joyously, unaware of Diane's disappointment the night before.

"It doesn't really hurt too bad, Mom," Marty said and hugged his mother, smiled up at her. She looked at the burn on his face and saw that although it was still ugly, red, and badly blistered, it was not infected. Hopefully it would not leave a scar.

She counted her blessings, said a silent prayer of thanks, and figured it was a small miracle in and of itself that the little fellow wasn't more seriously injured, receiving an electrical impact like that in the rain. Then she relaxed and allowed herself to be caught up in the children's enthusiasm.

During the bright morning the Rayner family opened their presents, and as they did, Kenny rang the doorbell.

"Look at this!" he said in awe. "You won't believe it, Marty, someone came and left a gift on our porch last night. I got a new compass!"

Diane and Marty exchanged a quick grin. Kenny obviously did not know who the gift was from and had not seen Marty leaving his house the night before. The two boys admired the compass and began talking about the adventures to come now that they had a new way of navigating their cherished meadow and woods.

As the boys talked, Diane noticed something strange. She watched her son carefully, studying him and trying to understand what was happening. Marty was not cocking his head when he listened to his friend. He actually seemed to be understanding Kenny with his deaf ear.

"Marty," Diane said and approached him, puzzled. "Does your hearing sound different?"

Marty shrugged. "I think so," he said. "Things seem louder than before and I don't have to work so hard to hear when people are talking to me."

Diane performed some preliminary hearing tests, and each time it seemed that Marty's left ear, the one that had been deaf since he was a toddler, was working now. When Marty was back at school following the holidays, the school nurse ran another check on his hearing. A report came home declaring that the hearing in Marty's left ear was completely normal.

Diane reflected on that memorable Christmas Eve, about the special gift and the electric shock Marty received as he ran back home that night.

"God, in all his mercy, saw a little boy whose gift came from the heart," Diane would say later. "In return, Marty's left ear, medically unfixable, was healed. That was a miracle only God could perform."

Later doctors confirmed the nurse's test results and suggested that the electric shock Marty received from the fence was somehow responsible for reconnecting damaged nerve impulses and restoring the boy's hearing.

Diane and Marty understood the incident as a true blessing. It had happened, after all, on Christmas Eve—the night when strange and miraculous things still happen to those who believe that with God all things are possible.

Touched by Heaven's Hand

𝒯here has always been something special about Bill and Becky Harter's fifth child, Scotty. The ten-year-old is quiet when his siblings are rambunctious; serious when they are silly. And above all, he is sensitive to spiritual matters and the feelings of others.

In some ways Scotty's personality makes Becky understand better the miracle of his life, and how but for God's healing touch he might not have lived to see his third birthday.

Becky knew nothing of the problems her son faced until shortly after his birth. The pregnancy had been normal, and on a beautiful fall day in Tempe, Arizona, in 1985, William Prescott Harter entered the world without complications. Almost immediately everyone called him Scotty.

Becky, a longtime nurse, had struggled with past pregnancies, and by the time Scotty was born she had suffered six miscarriages in addition to the births of her four older children. She knew for certain that Scotty would be her last, and in the morning after he was born, her arms ached to hold her newborn son.

Minutes slipped away and Becky began to wonder why Scotty hadn't been brought to her. When she was about to contact someone and ask about her baby, a nurse practitioner entered her room. The woman was a friend of Becky's, and as she approached the hospital bed, Becky saw that her face was stricken.

"Becky, I'm so sorry," she said. Tears filled her eyes.

Becky felt her heart stand still. "What is it, Sandy?"

The nurse practitioner paused for a moment. "I examined Scotty's charts and records. There's something wrong with his heart."

Becky searched for a way to make sense of the information.

"That's impossible. They checked him right after he was born and everything was fine."

Sandy shook her head. "They did some more tests. I'm sure about this, Becky. There's something very seriously wrong with his heart."

Becky studied her friend, knowing that she would not bring this type of bad news unless she was certain. Sandy had delivered a stillborn baby not long ago and Becky had helped her survive the grief. She was sure that Sandy would not suggest such a diagnosis unless it was true.

"Has the doctor seen the results?" Becky asked, her voice strained.

Sandy nodded. "He'll be here in a little while to talk with you. I thought you might want to hear it from me first."

Becky nodded and Sandy could see that she was partially in shock. The women hugged each other and then Sandy disappeared back into the hallway. Immediately she telephoned Bill and asked him to come to the hospital as soon as possible.

Shortly after Bill arrived, the pediatrician entered the room.

"I'm sorry to have to tell you this, but Scotty appears to have a large hole between the left and right chambers of his heart. Blood is passing abnormally from one chamber to the other," he said.

Becky tightened her grip on Bill's hand. "What exactly does this mean, Doctor?" Bill asked, his brow furrowed.

"It is very, very serious. Ideally, if the baby survives beyond his second birthday, we would do open heart surgery then to repair the hole. However, if he begins to show signs of respiratory failure or heart failure, we would have no choice but to operate right away. In that case, babies rarely survive."

Questions raced through Becky's mind: *What did we do wrong, God? Why is this happening to us?*

Meanwhile the doctor explained that the next series of tests would not be performed until Monday.

"Because you are a trained nurse, Becky, you can take Scotty home with you this weekend. But watch for signs of cyanosis, blue skin, difficulty breathing, drawing in the chest area."

"You mean he might not live through the weekend?" Bill sounded incredulous. Two years was precious little time but now it seemed the doctor doubted whether Scotty would live through the week.

"Yes, I'm afraid so. Many times children born with this type of heart defect don't live more than a few days." He turned toward Becky. "Do you think you can handle having him at home for a few days?"

Becky nodded absently, silent tears slipping down her cheeks. Bill put his arm around her shoulders and drew her near. The doctor bid the couple good-bye and left.

"What do we do now?" Becky looked up into Bill's eyes, searching for answers.

Bill sighed. "We take him home and do the only thing we know how to do," he said. "We pray for a miracle."

As they drove home with Scotty, Bill and Becky made a decision to keep the dreaded news from the other children. They also decided not to tell well-meaning friends and distant family members. Only Becky's parents, who were strong Christians, and six of their closest friends would know the truth about Scotty's heart.

"I don't want the children to be sad at a time when they should be joyously welcoming their new brother," Becky explained as she talked to her mother that evening. "And we don't need a lot of people grieving with us. Right now we want to pray for a miracle and expect that one will happen."

That weekend was a series of intense hours of prayer alternated with quiet moments alone with Scotty. On his first night home, Becky rocked her newborn son long into the early morning hours, whispering hopeful words of encouragement and telling him how much God loved him.

"Jesus will heal you, little Scotty," she said. And then in a silent voice she added, *Please God, know that we are standing on your promises. We believe with all our hearts that you will heal our son. Please, God.*

Then she stared at Scotty, sobbing softly and memorizing his face, wondering if that would be the last night she would ever spend rocking him to sleep.

Bill joined her before going to bed, and put a soothing hand on Becky's shoulder.

"He's going to be okay, honey," he whispered. "I really believe God is going to heal him."

Becky shook her head and cried harder. Her faith was weaker than it had ever been in her life, and she couldn't find the strength to believe as strongly as Bill did that things would work out all right for Scotty.

"I'm afraid I'm going to lose him, Bill. I understand how serious that type of heart defect is and maybe God wants him in Heaven for some reason."

Bill nodded. "I know, honey. But deep inside I have a feeling he's going to be okay. It's something I can't explain."

Becky sniffled loudly. "Good. At least one of us is believing. And, Bill, pray that I might believe it, too."

The next morning, Becky woke feeling as if a burden had been lifted from her shoulders. She checked on Scotty and found him sleeping peacefully, and suddenly her heart soared.

"As if God was trying to reassure me that you were right," she told her husband later that morning. "Scotty is going to be fine, even though it doesn't make sense right now."

On Monday morning, Becky bundled Scotty into a receiving blanket and she and Bill carried him into the office of the pediatric heart specialist. The man had been in to the hospital to see Scotty the day after his birth and had confirmed the diagnosis at that time. Now he wanted to run specific tests to determine the exact severity of the hole between the chambers of Scotty's heart.

Throughout the morning technicians performed a series of tests on Scotty while the Harters waited anxiously to talk with the specialist. Finally, they were called into an examining room where the doctor was going over the test results. His face was a mask of gravity as he put them down and approached the infant.

"How's he been acting this weekend?"

Becky smiled nervously. "Fine, actually. Nursing and sleeping well, his color has been normal."

The doctor nodded and donned a highly sensitive stethoscope. He listened closely to Scotty's heart, and then turned him onto his stomach and listened again, this time through his back. Once more he repeated this procedure until finally he stood up straight and sighed.

"All I can say is, I'm sorry," he said, shaking his head.

For an instant Becky felt the color drain from her face and she gripped Bill's hand. He's dying, she thought. The doctor's going to tell us Scotty's dying.

Instead, the doctor continued. "I would never, ever have made this diagnosis if I wasn't one hundred percent certain." He stopped for a moment, searching for words. "There is no explanation for this except that a miracle must have happened."

Becky caught her breath and waited for the doctor to continue.

"What are you saying, Doctor?" Bill asked, daring to believe the impossible.

The doctor glanced once more at the most recent test results. "This baby is perfectly normal. There's nothing wrong with Scotty."

Becky began to cry and clutched Scotty tightly to her chest. "Thank you, God, thank you," she muttered softly into the child's ear.

Bill struggled to find his voice, his eyes brimming with unshed tears. "Where do we go from here? Should we watch for any symptoms or have more tests done in a few months?"

The doctor lifted his eyebrows, at a loss for an explanation. "There simply is no hole between the chambers of his heart. It's disappeared completely." He smiled and ran a finger gently over Scotty's cheek. "All you need to do now is take him home and love him."

For months Scotty's case was studied by teams of specialists. Each time they tried to understand how a hole that had clearly shown up on tests taken at birth had somehow disappeared two days later. Finally, the case was recorded as without medical explanation.

Every now and then, when Becky watches Scott playing basketball with his peers or talking heart to heart with his father, she remembers how he almost missed out on life altogether. It's at times like those that she knows she has the only answer that makes sense.

"God heard our prayers and in his perfect will he answered us with a miracle. Our very own miracle baby."

Brought Back to Life

$\mathcal{S}$carlet fever hit the Bedford home in the spring of 1946. Rosemary and Bill Bedford lived in an old rambling farmhouse on the outskirts of town and the only medical attention they could afford was an occasional house call from the local family doctor.

"Looks like they all have it, even the little one," the doctor said grimly after diagnosing the Bedford's three daughters one morning. "I'll have to put a quarantine on the house and you'll need to care for the girls around the clock. Give them aspirin for the fever and keep them cool with wet rags. I'll check on you again in a few days."

The Bedfords were gravely concerned as the doctor closed the door behind him. Ellie, ten, and Bonnie, six, were old enough to withstand the vicious illness. But little Susie wasn't even three yet and her fever was highest of all.

"I'm not sure what to do," Rosemary admitted

tearfully, her voice hushed so the children wouldn't hear her. She looked into her husband's eyes and he saw the fear there. "I'm so afraid, Bill."

Bill placed his large, work-worn hands on her shoulders and did his best to soothe away her tension. "We'll just take it one hour at a time and pray that the girls get better quickly. Lots of people have scarlet fever, Rosemary. Everything'll be all right. You'll see."

The work of caring for three very sick children was overwhelming. They took turns working with each child, attending to their fevers and seeing that they were all drinking enough water.

But as the days wore on, Susie continued to get worse.

"Did you give her aspirin yet?" Bill asked wearily, finding Rosemary in the kitchen. One week had passed since the doctor's visit, and the older two girls were showing signs of improving. Only Susie remained desperately sick.

"Yes, is she hot again already?"

"Burning up."

Rosemary hung her head and quietly began crying, exhausted and discouraged that nothing seemed to be helping their youngest daughter.

Bill watched her compassionately and checked the clock on the wall. It was nearly eight o'clock.

"Listen, honey, why don't you go on upstairs and get some sleep tonight? I'll stay up with Susie and make sure her fever doesn't get too high."

Rosemary looked up and Bill saw that her eyes were only half-open. She waited a moment, thinking about her options, and finally she nodded. "You'll come get me if anything changes?"

"Yes. Don't worry about a thing. I'll give her some more aspirin now and then I'll sit right beside her all night. She'll probably do much better tomorrow."

Rosemary stood up slowly and kissed Bill on the cheek. "Thank you," she whispered. Ten minutes later she was asleep in bed.

Bill tiptoed into Susie's room and found the child curled up in her crib. "Susie," he cooed. "It's Daddy. Daddy's here now. Everything's okay."

He walked up to the wooden railing and felt her skin. It was dry and parched and even hotter than before. A burst of panic surged through him but he forced himself to remain calm. Gently he lifted her into his arms and sat down with her in a nearby rocking chair.

"Wake up, honey, I have some aspirin for you."

The child's eyes fluttered and Bill noticed how cracked her lips were. Her fever was raging and he worried that the heat might be dehydrating her body. He gave her the tiny pink children's aspirin tablets and a sip of water.

"Drink some more, baby," he said in a soothing voice.

"No, Daddy," she cried. "No more."

Then she was asleep again. She lay her head on his shoulder and fell asleep against him. Bill's upper body began to sweat from the intense heat of the child against him.

"Please, God, let her get through this," he whispered. Then he ran his hand gently over her hot forehead and began humming to her.

Hours passed and the aspirin seemed to have no affect on the child's fever. Bill began using wet cloths to cool her body, but still the fever raged.

After midnight sometime Bill noticed that Susie's breathing had begun to grow more difficult. *How will I know if this is really an emergency?* he asked himself. *At what point do I forget the quarantine and take her to the hospital? Help me, God.*

Then at 4:30 that morning, with everyone else in the house still asleep, Susie made a terrible gasping sound and suddenly bent over backward, contorting her spine so that the back of her head nearly touched her hips.

She made the gasping sound once more and Bill saw that she was arching backward in an attempt to breathe. Her airways seemed to have closed down, making it impossible for her to inhale. He carried her through the house as fast as he could, called the local doctor, and explained the situation.

"You need to get her to the hospital immediately," he said. "I'll call ahead and make arrangements."

The hospital was only six miles away so Bill raced to wake up his wife and daughters and the family drove as fast as they could with Susie in the front seat, still gasping for air.

"Dear God, help us," Rosemary cried, clinging to the girl and rocking her as Bill drove and silently committed Susie's fate to God.

Lord, you know how much I love my girls and you know how special each of them is to me and Rosemary. But things don't look good for Susie right now. I want you to know something. If you take our littlest angel, I'll still trust you. She belongs to you, after all. But oh, Lord, if you'll let us keep her for a while longer, I swear I'll do my very best to raise her right.

The hospital was still two miles away when the Bedfords began to hear a strange gurgling in Susie's throat. About the same time, she stopped trying to gasp for air and her lips began to turn blue.

"Bill!" Rosemary shouted. "She's not breathing." She shook the small child firmly. "Susie! Wake up, come on, honey. Breathe, Susie! Please breathe."

Bill raced around another corner and whipped the car into the hospital parking lot. He had barely stopped the car when Rosemary rushed from the passenger seat, carrying Susie in her arms, and ran into the emergency room.

The nurses were waiting and one of them took Susie from her mother and lay her on an examining table. "This child's dead," she shouted. "Someone get the doctor."

Rosemary screamed in her grief and watched in horror as the nurse tried in vain to find Susie's pulse. At that instant, a young intern came racing down the hallway and moved the nurse aside. He massaged Susie's chest and then listened to her heart.

"Nothing," he murmured. Then he repeated the procedure two times until finally he heard a heartbeat.

Without waiting he swept her into his arms and carried her into a room where he hooked her up to forced oxygen. For the next several hours he worked over her without stopping while her parents and sisters waited in the hallway.

Finally, the exhausted intern approached the Bedfords and slipped his hands into the pockets of his white jacket. "She's breathing on her own now," he said, offering only the hint of a sad smile. "But she has slipped into a coma. There is no telling how long before she'll come out of it. Or even if she'll come out."

Relief mixed with uncertainty flooded the faces of Bill and Rosemary. Bill stepped forward and shook the young doctor's hand. "The nurse said she was dead, Doctor. What happened?"

The intern nodded. "Technically, she had already died when your wife brought her in. She wasn't breathing and had no heart-beat. But I knew she was suffering from scarlet fever and that meant you'd probably been giving her baby aspirin to bring down her fever."

Bill nodded. "She's had it several times today, since her fever just kept rising. Every four hours just like the bottle says."

"That's what I suspected. You see, we're just learning about aspirin poisoning, Mr. Bedford. I've been doing research on it for the past year and I recognized her symptoms as being identical to what we will one day expect to see in a case of aspirin poisoning."

"Aspirin poisoning?" Rosemary looked confused. "But aspirin is the only thing that helps a child with scarlet fever. And we never gave her more than the correct dose for her age."

The intern nodded. "Normally there wouldn't be a problem, Mrs. Bedford. But sometimes a child will have a reaction, possibly when there is too much aspirin accumulated in her body, and then her fever will climb even higher."

He explained that as the fever increases, septicemia sets in— infection throughout the body. After that, the respiratory system can shut down under the strain and the patient can die.

"Is it common, Doctor?" Bill asked. "I've never heard anything about this in the past."

The intern raised an eyebrow and shook his head. "That's the amazing thing, Mr. Bedford. There hasn't been a single documented case of aspirin poisoning yet. Just speculation and research."

"But if you hadn't known what to look for . . ." Bill stopped in mid-sentence.

"She wouldn't have made it," the intern said quietly. "Thank God I was here tonight and I knew what to look for." He paused a moment and stared intently at the couple. "Normally I would have gone home hours ago but just after midnight something told me to stay a little later and work on my patient charts. Strange how things work, isn't it?"

He turned then and went back to check on Susie while Rosemary and Bill stared at each other in disbelief. Bill felt his eyes well up with tears and he struggled to speak.

"I asked the Lord to spare our little Susie tonight," he said, his chin quivering. "But I told him if he wanted to take Susie home I would let her go. It's a miracle, Rosemary, but tonight he brought her back to life so she could spend a little more time with us."

Rosemary nodded and collapsed against her husband, tears spilling onto her cheeks. Nearby, the older girls, too, were crying. "I thought we'd lost her, Bill," Rosemary whispered.

"God knows what he's doing, honey. You watch," he pulled away so he could see his wife's eyes. "She'll come out of that coma and she'll be just fine."

In the days that followed, Rosemary and Bill and another couple who were close friends of the Bedford family took turns sitting with Susie and praying for her. On the tenth morning, the Bedfords received a telephone call early in the morning. It was Susie's nurse at the hospital.

"Come down quickly," she said and Bill could hear the smile in her voice. "Susie's awake and she's asking for you."

"Is she all right?" Bill sat up in bed and waited breathlessly for the answer.

"Yes, Mr. Bedford. She's fine. But she'll be a lot happier when she can see her mommy and daddy."

Today, the miracle of what happened to Susie Bedford lives on. Her case is documented in the files at Children's Hospital in Denver as the first official incident of aspirin poisoning. Doctors still are not sure what the young intern did that night to save the child from advanced respiratory failure.

As for the Bedfords, Bill and Rosemary watched Susie grow into a beautiful young woman whose faith was every bit as strong as theirs. They remain thankful for her life, much as they were that dreadful night. And several times a year they send a donation to Children's Hospital in remembrance of a certain young intern who was placed in their path one freezing night in 1946 by way of a miracle.

The Greatest Love Is This . . .

*Y*ears before Melissa Phillips was diagnosed with terminal cancer, she was a healthy, strikingly beautiful teenager with eyes for only one boy: Jim McDermott. The two were in eighth grade when they met, and by the time they were in high school, they had fallen deeply in love.

"Honey, maybe you should go out with your girlfriends tonight," her mother, Sandy, occasionally suggested. "A girl your age doesn't need to spend so much time with one boy."

But usually Melissa wound up with Jim anyway. She and Jim ran with the popular crowd, staying out late at parties and causing her parents to wait up worrying about her. The Phillips had raised their three children to love God and be faithful to his plan for their lives, but Melissa had them concerned.

"If a boy really loves you, he won't ask you to compromise, sweetheart," Sandy would explain.

Then, when Melissa and Jim were seniors in high school, Melissa got pregnant.

"I want to keep the baby," Melissa said when she told her parents the news. "Jim and I both want to raise this child and be his parents."

Sandy's heart felt as if it might break for her bright, beautiful daughter, but she was thankful that Melissa had trusted her with the truth. "We'll do whatever we can to help you, honey," she said, stroking her daughter's hair. "Somehow we'll all get through this together."

Seven months later Melissa gave birth to a healthy baby boy and named him Christian. The child shared a room with Melissa in her parents' home for the first two years of his life. Then Melissa and Christian moved into an apartment with Jim.

"Melissa, if you and Jim love each other, then you can wait until you're ready to get married before you live together," Sandy gently told her daughter.

Melissa loved her mother and father deeply but she was determined to make things work out her way. She stopped attending church and seemed disinterested when her mother spoke of prayer or the power of scriptures.

"I already know all that, Mom," she would say. "It just isn't practical for me right now in my life."

A chasm was developing between mother and daughter, and one thing or another seemed to cause it to widen every day. It was a gap neither Melissa nor her parents were sure how to bridge.

Melissa and Jim had begun attending college and were earning high marks in all their classes. But Melissa's eyes no longer seemed to sparkle and the young couple's apparent lack of interest in their faith caused Gary and Sandy to pray for them each day.

Four years passed, and in the spring of 1994, Melissa and Jim were among the honor students who received their bachelor's degrees from the university. That summer, Sandy and Gary made a decision.

"We've been doing our best to accept Melissa's situation," Gary said one afternoon. "Maybe we need to do more than that."

Sandy nodded, stopping for a moment and staring into her husband's eyes. "I've been feeling the same way."

"I think it's time we really love them, spend more time with them and let them know that our love for them does not depend on their response to God's calling."

"We already love them, Gary, don't you think?"

"Yes, of course. But I mean let's really show them that love. And let's keep praying that God will develop a deeper love between them, one that will move them toward commitment. If that's not God's plan for them, we'll pray that they will part peacefully and go their separate ways."

Sandy nodded again. They had both been praying that way all along but it was good to talk about the situation. The split between them and Melissa had grown over the years and she believed her daughter felt condemned, judged for her behavior.

It was a feeling she could track back to her daughter's pregnancy. Prior to that time, Melissa had been a fun-loving, independent young girl with a sweet spirit. But after she got pregnant, it seemed that Melissa no longer valued herself the way she once had. Almost as if a light had been snuffed out in the core of her being. The transformation had been especially difficult for her parents.

Now Sandy agreed with her husband that she wanted Melissa and Jim to know how deeply they were loved, regardless of their decisions.

The plan was set in motion, and when Gary and Sandy weren't making plans to have dinner or a picnic with the young couple, they were busy praying for them, even fasting in their intense efforts to have God answer their prayers.

Summer passed and Sandy could feel the barriers that separated her from Melissa dropping. Love was the answer, after all. There was a closeness that hadn't been there for years and Sandy was thrilled with the change.

"You were right," she commented one morning before sharing

breakfast with Gary and their other two children. "All Melissa and Jim needed was an extra dose of love. I think the Lord is really working things out between all of us."

Then in September Melissa telephoned one evening with news.

"Jim and I are getting married," she announced happily. "We're thinking sometime in January."

"Oh, Melissa, that's wonderful," Sandy said, motioning for Gary to join her. "You've loved Jim for such a long time now. I know neither of you will be disappointed by this decision."

"You've been praying for me, haven't you, Mom?"

"Yes, of course, sweetheart. I've prayed for you since the day you were born."

"No, I don't mean like that. I mean you've been praying that Jim and I would do what was right in God's eyes and make a decision about our relationship. Isn't that right?"

There was a brief pause. "Yes, dear. I have been praying. Your father's been praying, too."

"Well . . ." Melissa seemed unsure of the exact words she wanted to say. "I just want to say thanks."

"Melissa," Sandy said, her heart soaring, "you don't have to thank me for praying for you. It's part of being your mother."

"I know, Mom, it's just that, well, I know things haven't been very good between us and, well, I wanted you to know I love you. And I'm glad you still pray for me even if I don't act like it." She hesitated. "Hey, Mom, do you think we could go shopping and look at wedding dresses one of these days?"

The healing continued strongly, and over the next few weeks, as Sandy helped Melissa pick out wedding invitations and plan the reception, the difference in their relationship was dramatic. The prayers she and Gary had uttered so often were being answered.

"For so long she's felt like the black sheep of the family," Sandy explained to Gary one evening. "Now she's finally starting to believe she's worth something. It's like watching a miracle unfold."

That fall Melissa joined her mother and grandmother on a trip to find the perfect wedding dress. There were several that were not right for one reason or another, but later that afternoon Melissa stepped out of the dressing room at a small bridal shop and Sandy gasped. The dress was simple and elegant, and in it Melissa was absolutely stunning. She looked at her reflection and admired the dress.

She's seeing herself as beautiful, on the inside and the outside, Sandy thought. *We have our old Melissa back with us again.*

Sandy flipped the price tag and saw that the dress was very expensive.

Melissa's face fell. "It's too much, Mom. I'll go take it off."

"You will do no such thing," Sandy interrupted, a broad smile filling her face. "That dress was made for you, and whatever we have to do, you will wear it on your wedding day."

Melissa stepped gracefully off the fitting room platform and hugged her mother. "You really love me, don't you, Mom? Even after all I've done wrong?"

"Everyone makes mistakes, honey," Sandy whispered, her voice too choked to speak. "My love for you will never be something you have to earn."

Six weeks before the wedding, Melissa learned she was again pregnant. Gary and Sandy hid their disappointment and promised to do everything they could to help in the pregnancy and delivery.

"Are you upset with her?" Gary asked after they learned about the pregnancy.

"I wish it were two months from now, but I'm not upset with her. She and Jim love each other, and nothing in their lives has happened in the right order. They're about to solve that problem, though, and I will do nothing but support them both in love."

Gary agreed and the wedding plans continued.

In the weeks before getting married, Melissa visited her obstetrician for a routine pap smear. She expected the results to come back normal, and when they didn't, she was stunned.

"I can't understand it," she told her mother. "I've never had an abnormal pap before."

"It's probably nothing serious but you need to get right back and have some more tests done," Sandy said. She was concerned but she didn't want to frighten Melissa.

That next week Melissa returned to the office for a biopsy.

"We should have the results in a few weeks," her doctor told her. Sandy had accompanied her to the procedure and she thought the doctor looked particularly concerned.

"You don't think it's anything serious, do you, Doctor?"

The man frowned perceptibly. "Let's just wait until the test results come back. We'll talk about it then."

The wedding was spectacular, and many of those in attendance were among the church members who had seen Melissa grow up. They knew of her choices and how difficult life had been for her and they had prayed for her alongside Gary and Sandy. When the couple exchanged vows, there were tears in the eyes of nearly everyone who watched.

Sandy and Gary held hands as they realized how many of their prayers had been answered that day. *Now if only Melissa would love God like she did as a child, if only she would trust him again,* Sandy thought. *Someday, Melissa, honey, someday.*

But the young couple's happiness was short-lived.

Three days after the couple returned from their honeymoon, Melissa called her mother, sobbing hysterically.

"Mom, the doctor's office called and, oh, Mom . . ." She struggled to keep from hyperventilating.

Sandy felt herself go numb with fear. "What is it, dear, what did the doctor say?"

Melissa tried to steady her voice. "Mom, he said I have invasive cervical cancer. He told me I have three months to live and that my only chance was to abort the baby."

"Honey, where are you right now?" Sandy was already standing up, searching her desk for her car keys.

"I'm at home. I already called Jim."

"I'll be right there."

On her way out of the church office where she worked as a

secretary, Sandy stopped in to see the pastor. She explained what had happened and the two prayed for healing and for the family's ability to deal with whatever was happening.

Jim and Sandy arrived at about the same time and by then Melissa had calmed down. She was sitting on the sofa crying softly when they walked in. Sandy looked at her and remembered the beautiful gown and the stunning young bride she had been only a week earlier. How could she be dying of cancer when everything about her was just beginning to live?

"Mom, I've made a decision," Melissa said and sniffed, wiping the tears from her cheeks. "I'm not going to abort this baby. I can't do it. I don't want to do it."

Sandy gripped her daughter's hand and squeezed her eyes shut. *God, help us know what to do next,* she prayed silently. *Please help us.*

"Whatever you decide, God will get us through this, Melissa," she said.

Jim took his wife's hand and wiped an errant tear with the other. He locked eyes with Melissa and gave way to his tears. "I love you," he said, his voice choked. Sandy fell into a chair nearby and wondered how any of them would survive.

The following week Melissa saw one of the top oncology specialists in the Pacific Northwest. The man also had a deep faith.

"Listen, Melissa," he said softly. "God loves you very much and he loves the child you are carrying. But if carrying the child to term would mean your death, our ethics committee would have to recommend an abortion."

"I just can't do it, Doctor," she said, fresh tears welling up in her eyes. "I want to know what else we can do instead."

"I understand. Well, let me explain something about your cancer."

He went on to tell her that there are two types of cervical cancer—one which remains in the cervix and one which is invasive, spreading quickly throughout the body into other organs and lymph glands. Melissa had the latter kind.

"I don't believe in abortion but in your case your life depends on it. You need to do it, Melissa."

When Melissa still refused to schedule the abortion, the specialist arranged for a surgery whereby doctors could remove all the cancerous areas they could see without hurting the baby.

"Now all we can do is pray we got most of it and wait. In another month you can have an MRI to see if the cancer has spread to your other organs," the doctor said. "You should know that the odds are high that it will spread. It is invasive and that type of cancer moves very quickly through the body."

Melissa nodded. "Everyone at church is praying for me, Doctor. If God wants me to live through this, I will. I'll see you next month."

The following month doctors performed an MRI on Melissa. She had decided that if the test showed no advanced cancer she would keep the baby and carry it to term.

"I could abort this child and still die of cancer," she explained to Jim and her parents. "If God wants me to carry this child, then the test will not show advanced cancer." She looked at her mother and squeezed her hand. "Please keep praying for me, Mom." She looked at her father. "And you too, Dad. I know God hears."

Whereas Sandy and Gary had initially gone through a mourning period after learning about their daughter's cancer, now that she was requesting prayer and seeking God's will in the crisis she faced, they began to experience a strange peace.

"I have a feeling God is going to work a miracle in her life," she explained to her husband. "I'm just not sure what that miracle will be."

The test results from the MRI came back the next day. There was no sign of advanced cancer. Melissa celebrated the news and found renewed hope in what seemed like the obvious power of prayer.

By then, Melissa was four months pregnant. Her doctor decided they would take the baby by C-section sometime during her seventh month.

"Your baby is a girl but she will have to be born prematurely. There is a chance she will have physical or mental handicaps," the doctor warned the couple during an office visit. "But that's the only way we can begin aggressively treating Melissa's cancer."

That week more test results came back. The doctor had tested the cancerous tissue removed during Melissa's initial surgery. What they found was baffling. The cancer cells had no hormonal sensors, which meant that during pregnancy they wouldn't grow.

"All I can say is that this must be a tremendous answer to the prayers you have received," the doctor told Melissa. "Normally cancer mushrooms during pregnancy because the cells are so sensitive to hormonal increases. But your cancer is absolutely immune to that process."

Melissa got home that afternoon and telephoned her mother. "The prayers are working, Mom," she said. "Only God can handle this one so please keep praying."

The doctor continually tested Melissa to see if the cancer cells were becoming active. When they remained dormant, he allowed Melissa to wait until just three weeks prior to her due date. At that point the baby's lungs would be fully formed.

The cesarean section was performed June 14 and was watched by a dozen doctors who were aware of Melissa's situation and wanted to see how badly the cancer must have spread during the pregnancy.

Instead, after the specialist delivered Melissa's daughter, he opened up her uterus and for a few breathless seconds did nothing but stare at her tissue. It was pink and healthy and showed no signs of any cancer at all.

Tears spilled from the doctor's eyes onto his cheeks and he cleared his throat. "Well, it appears that the invasive cancer has spontaneously, unaccountably disappeared," he said.

Doctors strained to get a look at the girl and each of them stared a moment longer than necessary, shocked by what had happened.

"Makes you wonder about miracles, doesn't it?" one of them whispered.

When the surgery resumed, the specialist removed Melissa's reproductive organs and scraped the walls of several areas where invisible cancer cells might have lodged. At one point she had been suffering with invasive, quick-moving cancer. Now there was nothing but a small, slow-growing cancer on her cervix.

"We got it all and I would expect she should live a long, normal life like any of the rest of us," the doctor explained to Jim and Melissa's parents in the waiting room.

"And just so you know," he continued, "I have no doubt that what's happened with Melissa and that precious baby of hers was the result of a miraculous answer to prayer. That isn't something you'll find in a medical journal, but God must have something very special planned for your little one."

Since learning that the child was a girl, Melissa had known she would call her Alexandra.

"You can pick the middle name," she had suggested to her husband. But by the time the baby was born, Jim had still not chosen a middle name for her.

Two days passed while Melissa was not permitted to see little Alexandra. Then finally the moment arrived. Jim carried the baby into the room and placed her gently in her mother's arms.

"Alexandra," Melissa cooed, running her hand over the infant's fuzzy blond head. "Hi, honey. I'm your mommy."

She looked up at Jim then and smiled, still drowsy from the medication. "Did you give her a middle name yet?"

Jim nodded and glanced furtively at Sandy and Gary, who were sitting off in the distance, allowing the younger couple to enjoy the moment by themselves. Jim held up a document for Melissa to read. It said that the child's name was Alexandra Savior McDermott.

"Savior?" Melissa asked curiously. "You gave her *Savior* for a middle name?"

"Well, I asked your mom and dad and they said they didn't

see anything wrong with it." Jim straightened up and stared deeply into his wife's eyes. "The way I see it neither of you would be here if God hadn't saved you both. So I named her after the one who let her live. From now on, in our family the name Savior will be more than a word. It's what God has become to me."

Melissa nodded, her eyes flooded with happy tears. She turned once more toward her baby daughter and kissed her on the cheek.

Later, Sandy shared her thoughts with Gary.

"I was watching them and I kept thinking of that passage in the Bible, you know, from the book of John," she told him. "The one that says there is no greater love than that which would lay down its life for another.

"Melissa did that, Gary. She risked her own safety for the life of her child. In the process she grew to trust God as she's never trusted him before. Most of all, she lived out a real-life lesson about the kind of love many of us know nothing about, the greatest love of all."

Drive-in Delivery

Once Susan Sebel passed the thirtieth week of her third pregnancy, she began to relax.

Whatever happens after this, God can get me through it, she thought.

Susan was preregistered at Cedar-Sinai hospital in Beverly Hills, and even if it was a hundred miles from her Antelope Valley home, it was an exceptional facility. Susan wouldn't consider having her baby anywhere else.

Giving birth was never an easy event for Susan. At the end of her first pregnancy, she struggled through twenty-six hours of intense labor before finally delivering a healthy baby boy. The second time was even worse.

Susan and her husband, Robert, had known that time that they were having a girl, so they decorated the nursery in their house a pink Minnie Mouse theme. Then, just before Susan's thirtieth week, something went terribly wrong and she lost the baby. The tiny girl was fully formed and Susan had endured fourteen hours of labor before she was born.

A year had passed since then and this time the Sebels were certain they were having a boy. ·

"Yes, there's no doubt about it," they had been told after an ultrasound revealed no problems. "Your little boy is developing just fine."

Susan and Robert went home that afternoon and talked about removing the pink from the nursery. They had always wanted to have both a boy and a girl and now the daughter they had dreamed of might never be a reality. Thankful about the pregnancy, they put away thoughts of a little girl and welcomed the idea of another healthy boy.

"Let's wait a bit before we redecorate the nursery," Susan said softly. There was a knowing look in her eyes and Robert understood immediately. Susan had weeks to go before her thirtieth week. There was still time for something to go wrong.

Weeks passed and the pregnancy showed no signs of any problem. The baby continued to develop perfectly through the thirtieth week, and when Susan was thirty-four weeks pregnant, she and Robert shopped for wallpaper and redecorated the nursery in bright, primary colors in anticipation of their newborn son.

"I'm still worried about that long drive," Robert confided to Susan one afternoon that week. "It's two hours even in the best of traffic."

He worked as a nurse at a local hospital, which did not have the sophisticated maternity ward available to them at Cedar-Sinai. Still, he thought it might be better if Susan delivered the baby locally so they wouldn't have to mess with the drive.

"Robert, I've prayed about this and everything is going to be fine," Susan reassured him. "Remember how labor is for me? Twenty-six hours the first time, fourteen the second time. I'd have time to deliver the baby in Phoenix if I wanted to."

"All right. But still I'm going to get one of those emergency delivery kits from work and keep it in the back of the car. Just in case."

Susan smiled and patted her husband's hand. "Okay, dear. If it'll make you feel better."

The days passed and finally it was the week of Susan's due date. When there were no contractions and no sign of the baby's arrival, the doctor made a decision.

"Today is Thursday. I'll let you go through the weekend, and if nothing happens, I'm going to induce you on Monday morning."

Susan agreed. "Am I showing any signs of labor?" She felt huge and uncomfortable and was hoping she wouldn't have to wait through the weekend.

The doctor shook his head. "Not really. Looks like another marathon labor session."

Susan sighed and returned home, comforted only by the thought that the baby would be born by Monday at the latest. When her back began aching late that night, she thought nothing of it. Backaches were part of being nine months pregnant, she told herself.

But the next day, Friday, January 13, she woke up at three in the morning and knew she was in labor.

"Robert," she whispered, shaking her husband firmly.

"What?" He was instantly awake, glancing anxiously about the room.

"It's time." She flipped on the bedroom light, picked up the telephone, and dialed her parents' house. They lived minutes away and Susan planned to leave her and Robert's three-year-old son with her father while her mother followed them to the hospital.

"How far apart are they, dear?" her mother asked.

"They're pretty strong, but I have plenty of time," she said. "Still, I'd rather be early than late, so come as fast as you can."

Minutes later she and Robert were belted into their Chevy Blazer and headed south on Highway 14.

"Oh, no," Robert said as he glanced at the gasoline gauge. "We're almost on empty."

Susan raised a wary eye. "Well, let's stop real quick. We don't need to run out on the freeway with contractions coming every eight minutes."

When Robert finished paying for the gas and returned to the car, Susan was grimacing in pain.

"Everything all right?"

Susan shook her head. "It's different this time," she struggled to speak. "They're faster and a lot harder. I think you better hurry, honey."

Robert nodded, his eyes wide with uncertainty. He motioned for Susan's mother to follow and he pulled out of the station. But after only a few minutes, he couldn't see her car and he pulled over so she could catch up.

They waited three minutes and Susan was beginning to double over in pain. "Hurry, Robert," she said.

"But your mother, I lost her and—"

"She'll have to find her way there on her own," Susan interrupted. "I need to get to the hospital. Now!"

Robert sighed and stared at his wife with pleading eyes. "Listen, honey, if they're coming that close together then we should go to the local hospital. At least have them check you out."

"No!" Susan was nearly in tears now. "If there's a problem, they won't be able to help me, and if I'm very far along, they'll make sure I don't leave."

She bore down, gritting her teeth until the next contraction passed. "Really, Robert, I'd rather have the baby on the freeway than deliver at a hospital that isn't Cedar-Sinai."

"Okay, it's your call." Robert pulled back into traffic and entered the freeway. It was nearly five by then and commuters were flooding the freeway headed for Los Angeles in what was the beginning of the morning rush hour. Fifteen minutes later they were stuck on Highway 14 in bumper-to-bumper traffic.

"I can't believe this," Robert muttered. "There's got to be a better way."

He steered the Blazer onto the shoulder and sped along past

dozens of cars until the space ran out. Then he merged back into traffic, crossed four lanes toward the median, and began speeding along that area.

"Robert, be careful," Susan shrieked between intense contractions.

"Don't worry about me," he said, keeping his eyes locked onto the road in front of him. "Think about the contractions. Tell me if anything changes."

Several minutes passed with Robert switching between the median in the middle and the shoulder on the right side of the freeway.

"Okay," Susan shouted, her eyes shut tightly against the wave of pain. "Something's changing. Robert, pull over now!"

He glanced up and saw that the Agua Dulce Road off-ramp was only a few hundred yards ahead. He veered the Blazer off at the exit and parked on the side of the road.

"Please, God, help us," Susan cried out.

She was nearly hysterical and Robert was desperate for some way to help her. Suddenly he forgot he was her husband, the father of the baby. He was on duty, a nurse in an emergency situation. When he spoke again, his voice was calm.

"I'm going to get the kit from the back of the truck and put the gloves on. Then I'll check you and see how far you're dilated. After that we can decide what to do next."

Susan nodded. Her forehead was sweaty and her eyes were still closed from the intensity of her contractions. Robert did as he'd said, and the moment he reached his fingers between Susan's legs, he felt his stomach drop. The baby's head was only inches from being born.

He grabbed the cellular telephone they kept in their Blazer for emergencies, but after a minute of struggling with it, he discovered that the batteries were dead.

"Great," he muttered quietly. Aloud he said, "Susan, everything's going to be all right. Just keep praying, will you?"

Robert glanced around and saw that they were in the middle

of a deserted area. *We'd be safer back on the shoulder of the freeway,* he thought. *That way we can find a call box before it's too late.* He drove the truck back onto the freeway and parked when he saw a call box along the right shoulder. Then he jumped out and called paramedics from the box.

"Don't worry, honey, we'll get someone here right away," he said when he returned to the truck. As he spoke, he adjusted Susan's position so that one of her legs was on the open window of the passenger door, the other on the dashboard. He moved her seat back so she was partially reclined and then he prayed for the paramedics.

"Robert, I'm going to die," Susan shrieked as another contraction hit her.

"No," Robert shook his head, trying to convince himself. "You and the baby are going to be fine."

A California Highway Patrol officer was the first on the scene. He blocked off a section of the shoulder so the other emergency personnel would have room to park and then he ran up to the car.

"How is she?" he asked, his voice breathless.

"She's crowning," Robert said calmly. "The baby will be here any minute."

Susan screamed upon hearing the news.

Robert explained that he was a nurse and could take care of her until paramedics arrived. The officer agreed and held a flashlight so Robert could station himself between Susan's legs and watch for the baby.

"Okay, now, honey, I don't want you to push."

"I'm not," Susan gasped, panting from the exertion of the contractions.

"Good girl. Breathe out during the contractions and force yourself not to push."

At that moment, paramedics arrived and ran to the Blazer.

"Okay, get back, sir," they said to Robert. "We'll need to get her out and onto a gurney."

"No!" Susan shrieked. "If you move me, the baby will fall right out!"

"I'm an emergency room nurse," Robert explained.

The paramedics glanced at each other and shrugged. "All right, we'll stand here beside you until the baby's born. Then we'll load them both into the ambulance."

Robert nodded. "You aren't pushing yet, are you, honey?"

Susan shook her head wildly. "No! I don't have to. My body's doing it all by itself," she screamed out in pain. "It's coming, Robert. The baby's coming now!"

In that final contraction, the baby slid from Susan's body and into the hands of her father.

"Susan you won't believe this. Our little boy is a little girl!"

Tears sprang to Susan's eyes. They were parked alongside a busy freeway during morning rush hour; there were paramedics and fire trucks and patrol officers all around them and she had just given birth in the front seat of their Blazer. But Susan couldn't have been happier. She and Robert had their little girl.

One of the paramedics rushed in and untangled the cord from around the baby's neck. Then he wrapped her in a blanket and whisked her to a waiting ambulance. The other paramedic worked with Robert to make sure Susan wasn't bleeding badly. Then they transferred her onto a gurney and up into the ambulance.

They drove quickly to the nearest hospital and Robert called Susan's father to explain what had happened. Thirty minutes after that, Susan's mother called.

"I'm at Cedar-Sinai and no one's seen or heard from the kids," she told her husband frantically. "I think there's been a problem."

Her husband laughed gently. "No problem, dear. Just an eight-pound little baby girl who didn't have the patience to be born in a hospital."

"My God, she had a girl! But where . . ."

"Born on the Antelope Valley Freeway, dear. Yes, and I believe God had a lot to do with it. Everyone's just fine. Now why don't you get back in your car and come home so you can meet your little granddaughter."

Two days later, Susan and Becky Ann left the hospital and returned home in perfect health. Seven months later, Susan learned that she was pregnant once more.

"This time, I'm going to induce labor two weeks early and book you a room at the hospital," her doctor joked. "Just in case there're any problems with the delivery. I'd hate for you to spend those last few weeks worrying."

"What are we worried about, Doctor?" Susan grinned. "God got me through a freeway delivery. There's not much left to worry about after that."

"Please Let Him Walk Again"

$\mathcal{T}$he morning of September 14, 1994, was much like other summer mornings in southern Arizona. September was monsoon season and fierce thunderstorms flooded freeways and side streets nearly every night.

Melissa Goodman thought nothing of the wet morning as she dressed two-year-old Andrew and prepared to leave for work. Life was busy at the Goodman house and there was little time to notice weather patterns. Melissa worked as a nanny from seven o'clock each morning through the afternoon and was thankful she could take Andrew with her. Keith, her husband, sometimes spent eighteen hours a day working construction sites throughout the city streets.

Then, when Melissa finished her job, she took Andrew to her mother's so she could attend classes at Mesa Community College. There were weeks when it seemed she and Keith rarely saw each other.

"Sometimes life seems like it's going too fast," Melissa had complained to Keith in the months leading up to that day.

"I know, honey, but it's temporary. You're working toward your degree and we both need to work so we can save up enough money to buy a house someday. God will give us the strength to survive this time in our life."

Melissa nodded. "I know. It just seems too fast sometimes."

That morning was no exception. Melissa, five months pregnant, raced out the door with Andrew under her arm and side-stepped puddles as she made her way to the car.

She buckled Andrew into his car seat next to her up front, then she slid in and fastened her own belt. She glanced at her watch and saw it was 6:30, the latest time she could leave and still be at her job on time.

"All right, little buddy," she said, tousling Andrew's hair and grinning at him. "Let's get to work, okay?"

"Here we go!" Andrew squealed. He loved spending time with his mother and felt none of the burden she carried in being so busy.

The roads were wet and water had collected along the gutters of most streets. Melissa turned out of her driveway, and several minutes later she headed east onto the busy street that she took every morning.

The traffic was heavy and at that instant a passing car sprayed water onto her windshield. The glare of the rising sun reflecting on the wet glass temporarily blinded Melissa and she gently applied the brake.

As she moved to flip her windshield wipers on, there was a violent impact and everything came to a sudden stop. Melissa could still not see out her windshield but she gazed around the inside of her car and realized that the frame had buckled. Her knees had slid under the dashboard and the steering wheel was jammed into her ribs.

"Andrew!" she screamed, staring at the toddler beside her.

He was still in his car seat but his head was limp, hanging

unnaturally onto the padded tray of his seat. Melissa tried to move toward him but she was stuck.

"Andrew, get up, baby!" she shouted.

The child remained motionless, his eyes closed and his face deathly pale. Melissa saw that blood trickled from the corner of his mouth and she slammed her hand onto her horn hoping someone would help them.

In seconds, a man opened the car door. "Paramedics are on their way," he said. "Don't move the baby."

"What happened?"

The man realized then the woman's vision had been blocked by her windshield. "You hit a city bus, ma'am."

"Oh, my God, is anyone else hurt?"

"No. The bus is fine. Let's just worry about you two."

Melissa tried to break free of her seat belt in a sudden burst of energy but remained stuck. "Turn the car off, please," Melissa shouted. "I'm afraid it might catch fire."

The man moved across Andrew and turned the key, cutting the engine of Melissa's car. There were sirens in the distance and he left to direct them her way.

Melissa struggled again to unfasten her seat belt but she couldn't find it. "Please, God, let Andrew be all right," she cried hysterically. "Please don't let him die."

Paramedics arrived and Melissa slipped into a state of shock. Her hysteria vanished and she answered their questions calmly and without tears. She told them Andrew's name and age and directed them to a bag that contained their address and phone number.

After a brief check, one of the paramedics began shouting orders. "He's unresponsive, arrange for a med-flight."

Minutes later Andrew was taken by helicopter to a local hospital while paramedics worked to remove Melissa from the car.

"Is he okay?" she cried, no longer calm. She felt a sickening certainty that Andrew was not going to survive.

"They'll do everything they can for him, ma'am," one of the paramedics told her. "Let's worry about you now."

Before she could respond, she passed out. Hours later she awoke in a hospital bed with Keith standing next to her.

"Honey, how are you?" He had tears in his eyes and he gently took her hand in his.

"I don't know." She tried to sit up and then winced in pain. "Where's Andrew?"

"Sweetheart, it isn't good," he said, his chin quivering.

Panic filled Melissa's eyes. She held up a single hand and shook her head violently. "Don't tell me, Keith. I can't take it yet. Let's talk about something else."

Keith stared at his wife for a moment and realized she was still in shock. He cleared his throat and struggled to find something good to tell her.

"The baby's all right. They did an ultrasound and everything looks fine."

Eventually they would learn that Melissa had broken ribs and numerous internal injuries but nothing life-threatening. In a few minutes, she fell back asleep.

When she awoke the next day, she desperately wanted information about Andrew. Again Keith was by her side and he sighed tiredly.

"He's in a coma, honey. They've done a CAT scan and can't find anything wrong with him."

Keith had been informed that since the tests showed no broken bones or damage in his neck and spine, they had removed Andrew's neck brace.

"Now we have to pray he'll come out of the coma," Keith said.

Melissa nodded and began what seemed like constant prayer that God would look after Andrew and let him come back to them the way he had been before the accident.

Two days passed and doctors were puzzled. They could not get any muscle response from Andrew's left side, even when they turned him and moved his limbs for him.

"Usually there would at least be some twitching to indicate

electrical connection between the muscles and the spinal cord," Keith was told. "But your son isn't showing any connection at all."

Finally, the hospital opted to perform another CAT scan. This time what they saw was shocking. There was a clean break between the second and third cervical vertebrae so that Andrew's spinal cord was completely unprotected. Even the slightest movement could have severed the cord and caused instant death.

"I'm afraid we need to get him to a specialist immediately," a doctor explained to Keith and Melissa, who, though still in severe pain, had been released that day.

Andrew was sent to St. Joseph's Medical Center, which had a division that specialized in spinal cord injuries. Five days had passed since the accident. He was examined immediately by a specialist.

The specialist explained that when the area of the spine between the second and third cervical vertebrae is injured the result is almost always death or complete paralysis. In addition, the doctor had spotted leakage from the fluid around Andrew's spinal cord.

"That means there is some kind of tear in the cord, and we have no way of healing such an injury. Paralysis almost always results."

He went on to tell them that of the small number of people who survive an injury similar to Andrew's, only a rare few will ever walk again. Especially if there was indeed a tear in the child's spinal cord.

"I'm so sorry," the doctor added. "His injury is very, very serious."

Melissa clutched Keith's arm for support and stifled a scream. *This can't be happening, God,* she thought. *He's just a little boy. Only a week ago he was running and jumping and throwing his ball to me. Please give us a miracle.*

"There is one chance," the doctor said then. Melissa and Keith stared at the doctor, willing him to continue.

He told them that he had developed a surgery where a metal

rod would be inserted into Andrew's back to connect his skull to the third vertebrae. Harvested bone material would then be placed around the rod so that the material would grow together. When it was completely fused, there would be a good chance of complete recovery.

"There are risks," he warned. "During the fusing time Andrew would be very vulnerable to injury, and even a slight blow to that part of his spine could be fatal. Of course, there is a considerable risk that he might not survive the surgery."

There was silence in the doctor's office for a moment.

"What are the other options?" Keith asked.

The doctor shrugged slightly. "Really, there are none. Andrew's injury is very severe and he will not regain any mobility or use of his limbs without the surgery."

Keith turned toward Melissa and saw her nod slightly. "We have to try," she whispered softly. Her eyes were watery and she squeezed them shut, forcing two tears to slip down her cheeks.

Keith gripped Melissa's hand more tightly and then turned back to the doctor. "Let's do it."

That night Keith contacted their church and explained the surgery.

"We'll have people praying for Andrew through the night and all day tomorrow," the minister assured him. "Our hearts will be with you, Keith."

Keith called his family and friends and asked them to pray, also. Finally, he dropped into bed and cried himself to sleep.

The surgery took place the next day and lasted fourteen hours. Up until the time of the operation, Andrew was still in a coma and completely unresponsive to any stimulation.

In the waiting room Melissa and Keith took turns praying silently and aloud together, asking for a miracle. As the hours passed, the Goodmans went through a roller coaster of emotions, first believing that everything would be fine and then crying together in fear that they might never see their little boy again. Other times one of them would break down and the other would take on the role of comforter.

"He's so full of love, Keith," Melissa said, wiping her tears. "I keep seeing his little smile and I can't stand the thought of never seeing it again. I don't know how I'll survive without him."

"Shhh." Keith pulled her close. "We have to have faith. He's in the best possible place for this type of injury. Everything will be all right."

The day seemed as if it would never end. Finally, late that evening, the doctor appeared and smiled warmly.

"The operation was a success. I've never seen such a miraculous difference before and after surgery of this kind."

"Oh, thank God," Melissa said, covering her mouth with one hand as fresh tears flooded her eyes. She hugged Keith and then stood to hug the doctor.

The doctor said that he had tested Andrew's electrical impulses prior to the surgery and found them to be nonexistent. After the surgery the same test showed a one hundred percent response.

"So he'll be able to walk just like before?" Keith asked hopefully.

"Let's just say I feel very optimistic at this point," the doctor said.

There was some concern because Andrew was still in the coma, but for the next two days Melissa never left his side. She talked to him, sang to him, prayed for him, and invited as many friends and family as the hospital would allow in to help stimulate him.

Sometimes Melissa would doze off, but then in a few hours she would wake and take the child's hand in hers.

"I love you, Andrew," she would whisper. And then she would sing to him the same song he'd heard since birth. "You are my sunshine, my only sunshine, you make me happy, when skies are gray. . . ."

On the third day after surgery, Andrew opened his eyes and glanced around the hospital room. He was unable to talk because of the machines and tubing, but the doctor celebrated with Melissa and Keith.

"He's passed one major hurdle. There will be more but this is a real landmark on the road to his recovery."

Another landmark came one week after surgery when Andrew's condition improved so that he was taken off life support. The days became weeks and finally a month later he was allowed to leave the children's intensive care unit and be transferred to another hospital.

Two weeks before Christmas he was given permission to go home. A neck brace stabilized his upper back and neck, since the accident had left him with no muscles around the broken section of his spine.

A week later the young couple noticed swelling in Andrew's head and rushed him back to the hospital.

"After a serious injury like this, fluid tends to build up in the skull," the doctor explained. Surgery was performed to place a permanent shunt in Andrew's head that would allow the fluid to drain without causing pressure in his head.

As he began to heal from the operation, he also began taking steps and moving about the floor.

"Look at this," Melissa said, pointing at Andrew one evening and grinning. "Keith, he's regaining his mobility. He's going to be all right."

Finally, in May, the doctor examined Andrew's X rays and determined that the bone material had completely fused around the metal rod.

"But there is something else I cannot explain. When he was first injured, X rays showed spinal fluid that had leaked from a tear in his spinal cord. Now the X rays show no fluid, no injury at all to the cord." The doctor scratched his head, puzzled. "Somehow the injury seems to have healed, and that's unheard of. Still, it's the only way I can explain his mobility."

Melissa and Keith hugged each other and smiled at the doctor.

"We prayed for a miracle, Doctor," Melissa said. "And now we know that God heard our prayers."

Today Andrew Goodman has almost completely recovered. He remains listed as one of fewer than a dozen people nationwide who have recovered from his type of spinal injury. As for the healed spinal cord, no explanation has ever been found except the one the Goodmans still cling to: Andrew is, in their opinion, a walking miracle.

Rescued from the Jaws of Death

*N*ot until the Johnsons moved into their new home in Fort Lauderdale did they realize what the sign said on their neighbor's fence across the street.

"Trespassers will be eaten," the white wooden sign announced in black letters. Someone had attached the sign to the wrought-iron fence surrounding the grounds of the home.

Hmm, Troy Johnson thought to himself. *Must be some kind of joke or something.*

But soon afterward the Johnsons realized that there was a large lion living behind the high fence. Along with that knowledge came the rumors that circulated through the neighborhood. No one knew the name of the man who lived in the house, only that he was believed to be an international drug dealer.

Whatever his situation, Troy sometimes caught himself envying the man. His home was more of a mansion than a tract house and he drove a slick black Rolls-Royce.

"What I wouldn't give to have a car like that," he confessed one day to his wife, Lisa. "Just goes to show you that making an honest living doesn't really pay."

Lisa was astonished and she clucked her tongue to the roof of her mouth. "Troy, I can't believe you'd say such a thing. You're already a success in the financial world and besides we have our two little boys and our faith. What more could you want?"

Troy didn't know how to answer his wife but he couldn't shake the feeling that he did, indeed, want more than he had. He had been raised in a Christian home but he had fallen away from his beliefs. He assessed his life and knew that he drank too much and worked too many hours and spent far too much time desiring his neighbor's Rolls-Royce.

Lisa, meanwhile, had tolerated Troy's increasing absences as part of his rise to success, and with it his desertion of the faith he'd once held dear. But she was concerned. Her approach to life was getting farther from that of Troy's with every passing month.

Lisa and the boys attended Coral Ridge Presbyterian Church in Fort Lauderdale and once in a while Troy joined them for a Sunday service.

"Good to see you again," Dr. James Kennedy, the pastor of the church, would say. "We'd sure love to have you at the midweek Bible study sometime."

Troy would nod absently, already looking toward the door. Four or five weeks might pass before he would visit again.

"I just don't get into it like you do," he would tell Lisa. "Don't hold it against me, all right?"

Lisa would sigh and wrap her arms around Troy's neck. "I'll just keep praying that one day you'll want to go to church with us like you used to. And that one day you'll understand why it's so important."

Troy was touched by his wife's words. After that he tried to make an effort to change. He drank less and stayed home more, and whenever their neighbor drove past in his Rolls-Royce, he reminded himself of the blessings in his life.

Still, his heart was not convinced until eighteen months later.

Troy, Lisa, and a friend were lounging around the Johnsons' backyard pool while three-year-old Bobby and seven-year-old Ty played in the front.

Suddenly the peaceful afternoon was interrupted by the shrill scream of a young child.

"Daddy, come quick!" Ty shouted. "The lion's got Bobby."

Troy raced around the corner of the house and saw the most horrifying sight of his life. A huge lioness was stretched across the front yard, its jaws firmly clamped onto the back of Bobby's neck. The child's body was limp and Troy could see blood seeping onto his T-shirt.

Help me, Lord, Troy thought. *Show me what to do.* He considered grabbing a knife and attacking the lion, but he wasn't sure he had enough time. Then suddenly he felt a clear direction and he knew he would have to approach the lion immediately if he was to have any chance to save his son.

Troy ran as fast as he could toward the lion and grabbed it by the jaws, struggling to pry them open. The lion's whiskers poked at Troy's hands like so many needles and he saw the animal's jaw clamp down tighter on Bobby's neck. At that instant he heard Lisa behind him.

"Oh, God, please help us," she prayed aloud. "Please God, please help us!"

Just then Troy pulled at the lion's jaw once more with a burst of strength he knew he did not possess. As he did, the lion's mouth opened easily and the animal slowly backed away.

Troy swept Bobby into his arms and raced into the house, where the couple's friend, an expert in handling medical emergencies, bought precious minutes by applying pressure to the gaping wounds in Bobby's neck.

When paramedics arrived, they rushed the child to the hospital, where Troy and Lisa waited anxiously for a report on his condition. Not long after their arrival, they looked up and saw the doctor, his face grim with concern.

"I'm afraid Bobby has suffered a very serious injury," he said. "His windpipe has been punctured and we'll need to do emergency surgery."

Crying quietly, the couple signed a release acknowledging that the surgery necessary to save Bobby's life could also be the cause of his death. When they were finished, Lisa telephoned her pastor, Dr. Kennedy, and the man arrived in minutes.

The pastor checked with the doctor as soon as he entered the emergency room and realized immediately the gravity of the situation. Dr. Kennedy had been in a number of emergency rooms with church members and he knew from the severity of the doctor's words that Bobby was barely clinging to life. Before praying with the Johnsons, Dr. Kennedy said a silent prayer of his own.

Lord, these people are in desperate need of a miracle, he prayed. *Troy's faith hasn't been strong for such a long time and you can use this to turn his entire life around. But please show your mercy and let their little boy live.*

Then he went to the couple and prayed with them until the doctor returned and spoke to Lisa.

"You can accompany him to the operating room if you'd like," he said.

Lisa let out a small cry and then composed herself as she stood to follow the doctor. Troy remained in the waiting room, sitting between Dr. Kennedy and Ty, who was crying uncontrollably.

"It's going to be all right," Dr. Kennedy told the older boy, placing a hand on his shoulder. "God knows your needs and he will take care of you. No matter what happens with Bobby."

The boy quieted some and Dr. Kennedy turned to Troy. They began talking and the pastor learned that Troy was not only desperately worried about his son, he was agonizing over the lack of attention he'd given his family and the way his faith had become halfhearted.

Troy recalled how Bobby had nearly died of an infection when he was only an infant.

"And now this," Troy told the pastor, wiping tears from his face. "I think of the way I've lived my life and I feel ashamed."

Lisa returned then and both men noticed a sense of peace about her.

"What is it?" Troy asked. "How is he?"

She sat down and took Troy's hand. "It was the strangest thing, Troy. I was walking down the hallway next to Bobby as they wheeled him into the operating room. And he was calmer than me. He was completely at ease, Troy."

Lisa's eyes grew damp but her face shone with hope. "Air was leaking from his windpipe and he could barely talk, but you know what he said to me?"

Troy and Dr. Kennedy waited.

"He said, 'Mommy, sing me "Jesus Loves Me." ' "

Troy's eyes widened in disbelief. Lisa looked from one man to the other and then continued.

"All he wanted was for me to sing him that song." Then she softly began to sing the words, her eyes dim as she remembered having sung them for Bobby moments earlier. "Jesus loves me this I know, for the bible tells me so, little ones to him belong, they are weak but he is strong."

As Lisa finished the song, Troy began to cry in earnest. He let his head fall into his hands and he told them in a broken voice how wrong it was that his own faith had been nothing compared to that of Bobby.

"I can't help but think that I don't deserve him," Troy said, sitting up straight and trying to compose himself. "I don't deserve any of you."

Dr. Kennedy put his arm more tightly around Troy's shoulders then.

"Do you want to pray?" he asked.

Troy nodded, and there, while his son was undergoing surgery to save his life, he prayed as he had never prayed in his life. He told God he was sorry about the way he'd been living, the way he'd abandoned his faith. He asked for forgiveness and for God to give him one more chance with Bobby.

"Please let him live, Lord. Please."

Dr. Kennedy pulled Troy closer and hugged him while Lisa held his hand tightly in her own. Appearing completely broken, Troy hung his head once more and sobbed.

As he did, Dr. Kennedy felt an unreal wave of peace and assurance. *The boy is going to live,* he thought. Then he looked at Troy and realized the life-changing effect of the day's tragedy. In the midst of the pain around him, Dr. Kennedy smiled gently. *There will be not one miracle here today but two,* he thought.

In a few hours the doctor returned with news that did not surprise Dr. Kennedy.

"He's one incredible little boy," the doctor said and grinned. "Earlier today I couldn't imagine how that child was going to live. But he did and I'm thrilled about it. He's going to be all right."

The doctor hesitated a moment and stared at Troy in amazement. "But as long as I live, I'll never understand how you were able to open the jaws of a lion. No one has that kind of strength."

Later Dr. Kennedy learned from the Johnsons exactly what had happened to Bobby. Apparently, the lion was prowling the grounds on the other side of the fence when she saw the children playing across the street. In one swift, powerful movement the animal leapt over the wall, tore across the pavement and pounced on the smaller of the two boys.

As the lion clamped her jaw around Bobby's neck, a single fang ripped into the child's trachea, bruising the carotid artery. Had the injury occurred even a millimeter closer to the artery, Bobby would have died within seconds.

"God has been very good to you," Dr. Kennedy told Troy when they talked later that week. "You must never forget how close you came to losing your little boy and how great the miracle God worked for you that day. He gave you the power to open the jaws of a lion so that you would believe in his strength."

Troy smiled gratefully, imagining for an instant the sight of the enormous lion, her jaws clamped around Bobby's neck. "I'm not the same man I was, Dr. Kennedy. Everything is different now."

As the years passed, the Johnsons worked through the legal issues involving their neighbor and his lion. Eventually the neighbor moved and the Johnsons heard that he had died in a plane crash.

But most important of all were the changes in Troy. In his desire to be closer to God he no longer felt envious of people who had more material goods than he. God became first in his life and he believed that time spent with his family was the greatest investment of all.

Some years later Troy came across a passage in the Bible, from 1 Peter 5:8 which he shared with Dr. Kennedy: "Be self-controlled and alert. Your enemy the devil prowls around like a roaring lion looking for someone to devour."

"That verse had taken on a special meaning in Troy's life," he told his pastor.

"I've learned firsthand about evil and how it really can be like a lion, devouring me and my family if I am not self-controlled and alert," Troy said during one of their conversations.

"But now I really know the one who stands between me and the evil one. He is the one who gave me the courage and strength to open the jaws of the lion and save my son's life."

Tiniest Miracle Baby of All

*J*ulie Kamps watched her beautiful eleven-year-old daughter twirl and leap into the air, her ballet costume floating gracefully about her knees. Julie locked eyes with the girl and the two grinned at each other.

Thata girl, Portia, Julie thought. *Lord, you sure made her a fighter.*

Julie smiled once more at her daughter, and then her mind shifted back in time. Back to a day when no one thought Portia would survive the first year of her life, back to a time when doctors thought she'd barely walk, let alone dance across a stage.

It was 1984 and Julie Kamps was expecting her third child. Pregnancy had not always been easy for Julie. Her first baby had died in the fifth month, and although her second pregnancy resulted in the birth of a healthy baby boy, she still wondered if this pregnancy would end with another miscarriage.

"Jacob was just fine," Ken reassured her as he played with their eighteen-month-old son early in her pregnancy. "I'm sure everything will work out fine this time, too."

Julie knew Ken was right, but still she was concerned about her unborn baby. The Kamps lived in Williams, Arizona, and Julie planned to deliver the baby at home with the help of a midwife. As long as she could carry the baby to term, the doctor did not expect any problems and saw no reason why she couldn't deliver at home.

Still, Julie prayed daily that the baby would survive the pregnancy and that God would give her the wisdom and peace to cope if problems developed.

As her pregnancy progressed, she developed a constant low backache. But Julie told herself this was normal, since most pregnant women have back pain.

One morning when she was twenty-four weeks pregnant, Julie was at work when she realized that she was having regular muscle contractions across her abdomen.

False labor, she told herself. *Don't worry about it.*

But when the contractions continued throughout the morning, steadily increasing in intensity, she telephoned her doctor.

"Sounds like Braxton-Hicks," he said, using the the term for false labor pains. "Rest a bit and they should stop."

But Julie had already had one child and she knew the contractions she was experiencing were too regular to be false labor. Also, they did not change or stop when she changed her activity—which would have been another indication that the labor might be false. That afternoon she decided to telephone her midwife.

"The back pain is getting worse every hour," she said.

"What about the contractions?"

"They're regular. I've been timing them."

The midwife was worried. "I don't like the sound of it. Drink some wine and lie flat on your back for the next few days. It could be early labor, and in that case you'll need to go to the hospital."

The midwife and doctor were located in Flagstaff, a forty-five-minute drive from Williams. Julie wanted to be sure she was in real labor before traveling that distance.

The following day the contractions were still coming, even closer together. The doctor called Julie and wanted her to be monitored in the hospital. She and Ken found someone to watch Jacob, and the couple set off for Flagstaff. Once she was checked in to the hospital, they attached her to a fetal monitor which confirmed that she was in true labor. She was given medication to stop the contractions.

"There are sometimes serious side effects with this medicine," the nurse explained as she hooked up the intravenous bag. "Just press the nurse's button if you experience anything unusual."

Julie nodded and then glanced at Ken with a look that said, *Here we go.*

"Are you okay?" he asked, taking her hand in his.

Julie shook her head. "I feel awful."

Ken prayed aloud, "Lord, you see us now and know our hearts' desire. We look to you to take us each step. We are yours and this baby is, too."

He looked into Julie's eyes. "Are you scared, honey?"

"No. I prayed about this; I asked God to give me a warning and now I'm here. Everything's going to be all right."

Ken yawned. He had worked hard that day and the stress of the situation had taken its toll. He sat down in the chair near Julie's bed and in minutes was fast asleep.

Almost immediately, the medication made sleeping impossible for Julie. Her heart began racing and she felt as if she'd had ten cups of coffee. Two hours passed and then three.

Suddenly she was unable to draw a breath. Forcing herself to remain calm she glanced at Ken, but he was still asleep. She opened her mouth to yell but could force no air through to make any sound.

Stay calm, she told herself. *You have some time, but if you panic, you're finished.*

She searched quickly for the nurse's button and pushed it.

Then she pinched the intravenous line to cut off the medication, praying the whole time. Ken awoke and saw that Julie was in trouble.

"Hey, someone get in here, quick," he shouted.

In a few seconds a nurse appeared and realized instantly that Julie was experiencing an extremely rare side effect to the medication. She unhooked the intravenous needle and placed an oxygen mask over Julie's face.

"Breathe!" she commanded.

Within ten minutes the situation was under control and Julie was breathing on her own again.

"That was too close," the nurse told Julie and Ken. "We've done all we know how to do here. We're going to have to get you to Phoenix. You don't want to have this baby now: It's too early; it wouldn't live. In Phoenix you'll have the best technology possible."

The doctor explained that the hospital in Flagstaff was not equipped to handle severely premature births. He wanted to fly Julie to Good Samaritan Hospital in Phoenix as soon as possible. As preparations for her transport were made, Julie and Ken were finally alone again.

Ken was quiet, his mind racing. *What'll we do with Jacob? And what about the business in Williams? Who'll take care of the customers? We have no insurance, no way to cover these expenses. How are we ever going to pay for all this and whose going to work out the details? Most of all, where are you in all this, Lord?*

Ken brought his thoughts under control and looked at Julie. "I think we need to pray," he said.

Minutes later Ken looked more at peace. "This is God's situation to handle according to his purpose," he said. "I just want to make sure you're going to be okay, at any cost."

"I'm not afraid," Julie said, her voice little more than a whisper. "Just sad. I've already lost one baby and now I'm going to lose another."

Ken shook his head. "But we made it through once; we'll make it through again. God was there then; he's here now. God has given us Jacob. He's enough. It's hard to see a purpose in all this right now. But God is in charge."

He assured Julie that he would ride with her to Phoenix and that whatever happened, they would take the situation one day at a time.

As the sun rose, Julie and Ken were whisked into a waiting ambulance and driven to the airport, where they boarded a small plane and flew to Good Samaritan Hospital. A technician performed an initial examination and checked Julie's labor by monitor. Afterward, a neonatologist met with Julie and did an ultrasound.

On the screen appeared a small body, perfectly formed. It appeared to be a girl, wiggling and even swallowing. Measurements were taken and the doctor announced, "Looks like a normal female of twenty-five weeks. If she was born today, she'd have an eighty percent chance of surviving.

"In some ways, that reaction you had to the medication was the best thing that could have happened," he continued. "Otherwise you wouldn't have been sent here."

Julie grinned. "A girl?"

Hope, here was hope, Julie thought. *Portia—the name the couple had chosen to give the baby if it was a girl—might just have a chance.*

The doctor nodded. "That's a good thing, because girls have a much greater chance of surviving a premature birth. But let's try to keep her inside for a few more months."

Throughout the next week doctors kept Julie on a different medication to reduce the intensity of her contractions. Ken returned home because things had stabilized. But one week after they had arrived in Phoenix, the contractions became markedly stronger.

"We're going to have this baby today," the doctor informed Julie one morning. "I'm afraid we're going to have to do a C-section. The baby's too fragile to undergo a regular delivery and she's under stress. Her heart rate is dropping."

Julie nodded, swallowing hard. "I want to be awake. Even if she dies, I want a chance to see her and hold her."

Julie telephoned her mother, who lived nearby, and asked her to come down; then she called Ken.

"It's time," she said simply, too choked up to continue. "Pray, Ken, and hurry."

Two hours later she was wheeled into the operating room, where Portia Suzanne Kamps was born. She was fourteen inches long and she wiggled furiously, trying to draw her first breath.

"She's a fighter," the doctor said.

Maybe she'll make it after all, Julie thought.

Although she was long for a baby of twenty-six weeks, Portia weighed just one pound, twelve ounces. She was whisked immediately to the neonatal intensive care unit, where she was put on a ventilator inside an isolette.

"Why is she so red?" Julie asked one of the nurses.

"You're seeing all her capillaries," the nurse replied. "She has so little skin at this point, Mrs. Kamps."

Ken arrived later and the couple celebrated the fact that Portia was fighting for her life. Three days later, when Julie was released from the hospital, Portia was still gaining ground.

"I really think she's going to be okay," Julie told Ken while she hugged Jacob that afternoon. "Perhaps God has a special plan for our little girl."

Doctors told the Kamps that Portia would need to stay in the hospital for three months or longer. The couple agreed that Jacob and Julie would stay with Julie's mother, just minutes from the hospital. Ken would reluctantly return to Williams and his business, four hours north, and visit on weekends.

Weeks passed and Julie spent hours each day sitting by Portia's side and praying for her. A brief sponge bath in the isolette and the holding of her tiny hand was all the contact allowed for weeks.

Julie watched as the tiny infant tried to kick away the wires and tubing that surrounded her.

"That's a good girl, Portia," Julie would whisper. "Keep fighting, honey. Keep fighting."

Julie learned that the neonatal intensive care unit at Good Samaritan Hospital was a busy place. Never did more than a few days go by without the ward experiencing the death of one of its more than sixty premature infants. But Portia continued to gain precious ounces and fight for survival, wrapped in plastic wrap that acted as skin until her own began to grow.

Finally, after four weeks, Ken and Julie got to hold Portia for the first time. She was wrapped up so well that all they could see was a series of tubes and blankets. It was the most emotional five minutes of their lives. No one spoke for the tears.

Often premature babies die as a result of infection that has set in because of the invasive measures necessary to keep them alive. Several times Portia fought off life-threatening infections, and through it all Julie and Ken and nearly everyone they knew continued to pray.

Julie clung to the Bible verse from Philippians 4:6–7, and repeated it often in her mind.

"Do not be anxious about anything but in everything by prayer and petition, with thanksgiving, present your requests to God. And the peace of God which transcends all understanding will guard your hearts and your minds in Christ Jesus."

"Lord, at first I was resigned to losing her," Julie would pray as she watched over her struggling infant. "But now that she's lived this long, please bring her through, please let her come home. She's your child first. You love her even more than I. Please help me to trust in that and keep my heart and mind in you."

One nurse, Kelly, took a special interest in Portia and liked to say the infant was her adopted daughter. Kelly had lost a premature infant at the twenty-fourth week of her pregnancy, just six months earlier. The baby had looked a lot like Portia.

Kelly would watch while Julie and others came to pray over Portia, and her eyes would well up with tears.

"Portia is our little miracle baby," she would say. "Nothing's going to happen to her."

Finally three months had passed, and Portia's weight had climbed to five pounds. At that point her body systems were also functioning on their own—a necessity before a premature baby can leave the hospital.

"She can go home now," the doctor told Julie and Ken. "But the risks are far from over."

He warned that premature babies can suffer from retardation, seizures, and a number of other ill effects. Cerebral palsy is the primary concern. When a baby is premature, even a slight jarring motion can cause the brain to bleed, resulting in nerve damage or cerebral palsy.

In Portia's case, a sonogram had detected a low-grade bleed during her time in the hospital, so the Kamps knew to look for cerebral palsy. She would need a physical therapist to monitor her condition weekly.

In addition, babies like Portia are very likely to stop breathing in their early months and sometimes years. Portia would need to be hooked up to a machine that would monitor her heart and breathing and alert Julie and Ken if she had problems. Usually the babies need only to be nudged to begin breathing again on their own but the situation can be life-threatening.

The months passed and became years. Until she was two, Portia had numerous incidents where she stopped breathing, but each time she was able to start again on her own.

As she developed, Julie watched for signs of cerebral palsy, and when the child was a toddler, it became apparent that she had trouble with gross motor skills on her left side.

"Portia is truly a miracle baby," the doctor told Julie and Ken at one of their visits that year. "She has no sign of seizure or heart trouble. But she does show signs of cerebral palsy on her left side."

Julie and Ken discussed the situation later that night and

agreed that whatever difficulty Portia might need to overcome, they would treat her like any other child.

"God saved her for a reason," Julie said, thankful that Portia had been seeing a physical therapist since birth. "She's got the will and determination to do whatever she wants in this life."

Indeed, as the years passed, the doctor's preliminary diagnosis proved true. Portia did indeed have slight cerebral palsy on her left side, a condition that would make walking difficult and impair her sense of balance. At first doctors wondered whether she would be able to walk without the aid of a walker, or take part in even simple childhood activities, such as riding a bicycle.

But with every obstacle, Portia fought to overcome. She and her younger sister, Salem, developed a close friendship and never did her cerebral palsy keep the two from playing together.

"God made you special, Portia," Julie would tell her daughter. "He has a plan and a purpose for your life. Your cerebral palsy isn't a problem or a restriction. It's a reminder of how blessed you are to be alive."

Julie had a reminder of her own, of the blessing that was Portia's miraculous existence. When Portia was two and no longer needed her heart monitor, the Kamps returned the machine to the hospital. Not long after, they purchased a microwave oven that beeped exactly as the heart monitor machine had when Portia was in trouble.

The sound was so much the same that Julie would never hear the beep of her microwave without remembering the panic that sound had once caused. Now the sound reminded her to be thankful for Portia's survival.

Julie realized that the music had stopped and the ballet number was finished. Portia smiled graciously at the audience and swept into a delicate curtsy. Moving a little more slowly than the other girls, she made her way off stage to prepare for the next number.

"That's my little miracle girl," Julie whispered, her eyes dancing with joy. "Keep fighting, Portia. Keep fighting."

Angel in the Intersection

$\mathcal{S}$ix-year-old Stephen Stoner watched as his little friend ran dangerously across four lanes of busy traffic and jumped up onto the opposite curb unscathed.

"Come on," the boy yelled to Stephen.

Stephen looked behind him at Ellen, the sixth-grade neighbor girl who usually walked him home from school. She was talking to her friend and momentarily unaware of the younger children.

Stephen looked back toward his friend. *If he can do it, I can do it,* he thought. Then, without looking for traffic, he darted into the street.

Suddenly Ellen screamed and Stephen froze in the middle of the road. A car traveling forty miles an hour was just a few feet from hitting him. He tried to outrun the car but it was too late.

"No!" he screamed. And then there was a sickening thud.

Stephen Stoner had never been a difficult child. He was raised by parents devoted to God and to raising well-loved, well-trained children. Stephen and his younger sister, Sheri, attended church each week with their family and had been taught since their earliest memories about God and prayer and the power of faith.

Still, there were times when Stephen's young faith did not seem to help him. Especially at night, when Stephen was terrified to sleep alone.

Finally one night his mother placed a soothing hand on his shoulder and sighed softly. "Stephen," she said, "there's nothing to worry about. You might feel you are alone but you are not. God has placed a guardian angel by your side to watch over you while you sleep and to protect you by day. You have nothing to be afraid of."

Stephen was not completely convinced, but for the next week he thought a great deal about guardian angels and whether he did, indeed, have one. Each morning that week, like other weeks, his mother would drop him off at the public school he attended in Indianapolis. When school was over, Ellen and her younger brother—Stephen's friend—would walk him home.

But that afternoon, the girl was walking with one of her friends and was not paying much attention to the boys. Now, she watched in horror as Stephen was hit hard by the fast moving car. His small body flew into the air and he came down headfirst onto the pavement. Then he lay very still.

"Quick, someone call an ambulance," Ellen screamed. A passerby rushed off to make the phone call as a crowd of people gathered around. Within minutes an ambulance arrived at the scene, and not long afterward Stephen's mother appeared.

"He's conscious," one of the paramedics shouted. Then in a softer voice he mumbled, "This is incredible. The kid shouldn't even be alive."

Stephen lay on the ground, not moving, and trying to figure out what had happened. He remembered being hit and flying through the air. But when he hit the ground, there was no pain.

Almost as if someone had carried him through the air and then set him gently down on the pavement. He looked up and saw a circle of people working on him.

"Check his pulse," someone shouted. "Check the reflexes."

"Don't move him yet," another cried. "Let's check for head injuries."

He could see his mother, standing nearby with tears running down her cheeks. He smiled at her and hoped she wouldn't be too mad at him. After all, he'd been told a hundred times never to cross a street without an older person to help him.

He looked at the others around him and suddenly he gasped. There, hovering directly over him and gazing into his eyes, was a gigantic man with golden hair. The man was smiling and Stephen understood by the look on his face that he was going to be all right. As the man faded from view, Stephen's mother stepped closer.

"Stephen, are you okay?" she cried. "Honey, answer me."

Stephen looked toward her and grinned. "I'm fine, Mom. I saw my guardian angel."

A paramedic pushed her gently back from the scene. "He's in shock, ma'am. He's suffered a very serious blow and we're sure he has internal injuries. We have to get him to a hospital right away."

They placed the injured child onto a stretcher and strapped him down. "He could have back and neck injuries, any number of problems," another paramedic explained to Stephen's mother. "You can ride in the ambulance if you'd like."

As the boy and his mother left in the ambulance, police and firemen still on the scene examined the spot where the boy had lain.

"No blood," one of them said.

"Yeah," another man said, approaching and shaking his head. "Witnesses said the car was moving at forty plus and the boy sailed through the air. Came down on his head and there's no blood."

"I was thinking the same thing. Never seen anything like it."

At the hospital, doctors did a preliminary check to determine whether Stephen had feeling in all parts of his body.

"Look at this," one of the doctors said, running a hand over the boy's smooth legs and arms. "He doesn't have a single scratch on him."

"Didn't he get hit by a car?" The nurse assisting him was also puzzled by the boy's appearance.

"Yes. A small child like this, hit straight on by a car moving at forty miles an hour. Should have been dead at the scene. And I can't even find a bruise where the car made contact with him."

Within an hour the doctor had the results to a dozen different tests and he was stunned at what he saw. The tests were completely normal. The boy was neither scratched nor bruised and he had absolutely no internal injuries.

"My guardian angel saved me," Stephen explained, as the doctor grinned at him in amazement. "God was watching over and keeping me safe."

The doctor shrugged. "That's as good an explanation as any," he said. "I'll sign the papers so you can go home."

Today, Stephen is twenty-five and remembers the incident as if it were yesterday. After the accident, his young faith became vitally real, propelling him through his teenage years and into the only career path he could imagine taking.

He still enjoys telling the story to the young people he works with—in his job as youth pastor for First Assembly of God Church in Hartselle, Alabama.

EIGHTEENTH LITTLE ANGEL

The Miracle of Mary's Life

*P*aul and Jeannie French had spent three years battling infertility and praying for a child. So in spring 1993, the Oak Park, Illinois, couple rejoiced when Jeannie learned she was expecting a baby.

At first the pregnancy went along normally. But when four months had passed, Jeannie went in for routine testing and received the first warning that something might be wrong.

"The good news is that you seem to be carrying twins, one boy, one girl," the doctor explained. "But I'm concerned about the little girl. She is too small for her gestational age and she doesn't seem to be developing properly."

Jeannie glanced at Paul and then back toward the doctor. "I'm sure it's nothing," she said. "She'll be fine, Doctor."

"Let's do some more testing. Just to be sure."

During the next four weeks, Jeannie learned that

the female twin she was carrying had developed encephalocele, a severe birth defect in which most of the brain develops outside the skull in a sac at the base of the neck.

"I'm sorry," the doctor said simply after delivering the blow one afternoon. "There's nothing we can do."

Paul French studied the doctor, hoping there was some ray of hope that might still exist for his unborn daughter. "There isn't anything that can be done? Surgery, something?"

The doctor shook his head. "This condition is fatal because any distress to the brain stem causes death immediately in most cases. Babies with this type of defect will never have any protection for their brain stem since it has developed outside the protection of the skull."

He went on to say that even if the baby did survive for a short while, she would have no chance of any intellectual development.

Jeannie hung her head and allowed the tears to come. *Help us, God,* she prayed silently. *Work a miracle in our little girl's life.*

The doctor cleared his throat and shifted uncomfortably. "I'd suggest we perform a selective abortion to take care of the problem," he said. "That way there would be plenty of fluid and room for the other twin to develop."

Jeannie wiped her tears and stared at the doctor. "You mean you want us to abort our little girl?" she said, astonished.

"Mrs. French, she isn't going to live anyway. This would make it easier for everyone. There's no reason why you should have to go through the trauma of carrying two babies only to have one of them die at birth."

Jeannie stared at her husband and shook her head in disbelief. "Doctor, I can feel my little girl kicking. I know which side of my womb she is lying on and when she sleeps and wakes up. She may not have a very long life but she will have a safe and comfortable one. Abortion is out of the question."

Paul nodded. "I suppose we'll need to talk with some specialists about the specifics of the birth."

"All right." The doctor shrugged. "But I can see no reason at all to carry this baby to term."

The couple left the office in tears, and almost immediately Jeannie began trying to resolve the dilemma they were suddenly a part of.

"Let's name her Mary Bernadette," Jeannie suggested on the ride home. "St. Bernadette was a very sickly child just like our little girl. But God had a plan for her life, anyway."

Paul nodded, swallowing a lump in his throat. "Let's get everyone we know praying for her."

In the next few weeks Jeannie and Paul made phone calls to dozens of people, who in turn promised to call others, so that in time hundreds of people from churches across the country were praying for Mary Bernadette.

"Pray for her to be healed," Jeannie would ask. "And please pray for her safe delivery and continued health."

Next, Jeannie researched Mary's condition at Loyola Medical Center and learned about doctors and support groups that specialized in neural defects. She met with neonataligists, talked to neurosurgeons, and faxed sonogram reports wherever anyone was interested.

"You need to rest more, Jeannie," Paul reminded her gently one evening. "You're taking this on as if you could fix the problem yourself."

Jeannie nodded. "I want to do everything I can to help her, Paul. You understand, don't you?"

"Of course. But I've been thinking a lot about Mary. It's like someone is trying to remind me that sometimes God has a plan different from our own."

Jeannie understood and never during her pregnancy did she blame God for allowing Mary Bernadette to develop a birth defect. Still, she had absolute confidence that he would grant her a miracle and heal her unborn twin.

By the time she was six months pregnant, the twins had found permanent places on either side of her abdomen. Ultrasound tests showed which side Mary Bernadette was on, and Jeannie learned to recognize when the babies were awake. She would spend hours talking to her children and praying aloud for them.

"God has a plan for you, little Mary Bernadette," Jeannie would say. "Don't give up, honey. Everything is going to be okay."

About that time, Jeannie quit working so she could stay home and allow her body to rest. Specialists had told her that additional rest might make the difference in whether Mary Bernadette survived the pregnancy, or died weeks prior to delivery.

During those weeks, there were times when Jeannie pondered the irony of Mary Bernadette's situation. After all, Jeannie had been active in the fight against abortion for more than a decade. Now she was faced with a situation that many people had used as a hypothetical when debating the abortion issue across the country.

Jeannie was raised in a family where life was a precious commodity. It came as no surprise to those who knew her when she became politically active in college, in a number of ways that, in her opinion, were completely harmonious. She placed bumper stickers on her notebooks and was vocal as both a feminist and a pro-life advocate. Eventually, her convictions led her to a position as president of the National Women's Coalition for Life.

"I am for the rights of all human beings," she would say. "Pro-life encompasses not only the unborn, but also the elderly, the handicapped, the mentally ill. Anyone whose right to life is in jeopardy."

Now, as she prayed for a miracle for Mary Bernadette, she felt no less certain that the baby was worthy of life. But gradually, as the weeks wore on, tests showed that the sick twin's defect was even more serious than doctors had first thought.

"We doubt very much that she will survive the pregnancy, Mrs. French," the doctor said. "We'll monitor you every week to be sure she has a heartbeat."

Week after week Mary Bernadette survived. By the end of Jeannie's second trimester, she and Paul had a highly trained neonatal team scheduled to deliver the twins by cesarean section, since labor would be fatal to little Mary.

About this time, friends of the French's suffered a tragedy similar to the one they knew they were about to face. The couple had celebrated the birth of their son that month only to learn that he had a fatal heart condition. Without a valve transplant, he would die. The baby was fourth on the waiting list when his heart succumbed and stopped beating.

When Jeannie and Paul learned of the situation they sorrowed with their friends, but did not see a connection between their friends' situation and that which they were experiencing in their own lives.

"We need to keep praying for a miracle," Jeannie would say. "God will heal Mary and everything will be fine. I know he wants the best for us."

Then, when Jeannie was nearly eight months pregnant, she was sitting in church one morning when she was overcome with the thought that she was praying with the wrong intentions. Suddenly she heard what seemed to be a voice of authority telling her to pray for peace, not miracles. The feeling came over her again that evening as she lay in bed, feeling her twins move within her and thinking about the future.

"All right, Lord," she prayed quietly. "I will pray for peace and acceptance. If there is a reason why this has to be, then I will trust you."

In the next six weeks she focused her energy in a different direction. If Mary were to die at birth, then she and Paul would need help dealing with their loss. She contacted organizations that dealt with the loss of a child in multiple births, and others that helped parents handle the death of a young child.

There was one more thing. She talked with Paul one night, and the next morning she called the Regional Organ Bank of Illinois. She explained Mary's situation at length and recalled the death of their friends' son.

"We want our little girl to make the difference in another child's life," she said finally.

Jeannie was told that it is very difficult to find donors for infants in need of a transplant.

"When an unborn child develops life-threatening abnormalities, the majority of those pregnancies are terminated," she was told. "And when a child dies unexpectedly at birth or shortly after, the parents are often too traumatized to consider organ donation."

Jeannie laid her hand on her extended abdomen and knew they had made the right choice. Mary Bernadette's life would have a purpose; now she was certain.

Finally, the morning of December 13 arrived and Jeannie and Paul drove to West Suburban Hospital in Oak Park for the scheduled cesarean section. They had mixed emotions, knowing that Mary would not live long outside her amniotic sac.

As the doctor prepared her for the surgery, Jeannie stared at him, her face pensive.

"Little Mary is so safe and comfortable we were wondering if maybe you could just take William out and leave her in."

The doctor glanced ruefully toward Jeannie and understood her feelings. "How long should we leave her in?"

"Two or three years," Jeannie said, as she smiled sadly through her tears.

At 9:20 that morning William was delivered and let out a healthy cry. A minute later, Mary Bernadette was placed protectively in Paul's arms as doctors worked to stitch up Jeannie's abdomen.

"It's much worse than we thought," the neonatologist said quietly as he examined Mary. "She's dying."

Paul nodded and smiled tearfully at both his parents and Jeannie's parents, who had flown into Chicago so they could have a chance to hold Mary before she died.

"You can hold her if you like," he said.

Jeannie's mother took Mary gently in her arms. The child's eyes were open and she gazed into the older woman's face.

"Your great grandmother died not too long ago, little Mary," the woman said softly, nuzzling close to the infant. "We called her Bubba and I want you to sing to her when you meet her up in Heaven."

Then the woman launched into a traditional Slavic lullaby, singing as tears streamed down her cheeks. When she was finished, she allowed the other grandparents to hold Mary, each in turn telling the baby how much they loved her and that they would see her one day in Heaven.

The medication and recovery from surgery made it impossible for Jeannie to hold her right away, so Paul cradled Mary in his arms when the grandparents had had their turns.

"Mary, we will always love you," Paul whispered into the deep blue eyes of his little girl. "You will always be a part of this family and someday we'll all be together again."

Mary moved slightly and kicked off her receiving blanket. Several nurses standing nearby glanced at one another in surprise. Four hours had passed and still the infant was alive, defying medical understanding of the severity of her condition.

Finally, six hours after she was born, Mary gazed once more into her father's eyes and drew her last breath. Shortly afterward, Jeannie's medication wore off and she awoke. Only then did she get to hold Mary.

"Watch over us from Heaven, little one," Jeannie cried softly. "We will never forget you."

Two days later, Jeannie and Paul were notified by the organ bank that Mary's heart valves had been used to save the lives of two critically ill children in Chicago. The next day family members held a memorial for Mary Bernadette, a service that Jeannie was unable to attend because of her grief.

Weeks passed before Jeannie could talk about Mary with anyone. Only then, after hours of prayer for peace and acceptance, did she reach several conclusions about Mary's short life.

"Children aren't supposed to die," she said later. "When a child dies, it causes everyone to change their perspective and appreciate each tiny moment of life. It resets our priorities and forces us to cash in on the insurance policy of having faith in God."

Today Jeannie and Paul feel certain that Mary's short life is the reason they so deeply appreciate each day with their son, Will. Jeannie also devotes some of her time to helping other parents find peace in the tragedy of losing a child.

"The best we can hope for with any of our children is not the kind of career they choose or where they will live or how much money they will make," Jeannie tells people when she talks about Mary.

"The best we can hope for with our children is that they make it to Heaven. As for us, one of our children is already safely home. Not only that, but in passing through this world she gave life to two other children.

"How many of us can say that, even after living a hundred years?"

For the Love of Katy Belle

*T*he fleas had been terrible in Central Arizona that summer, but until September Sherri Reed had managed to keep them out of the house. She was an animal lover and her children shared that love. At different times the Reeds' house had been home to a rabbit, a kitten, a dog, a snake, and an iguana.

That summer the rabbit and snake were gone, but the Reeds had a new kitten, and Sherri's twin daughters loved her more than any pet they'd ever owned.

"She's a little crazy, isn't she, Mom?" ten-year-old Sarah would say, tilting her freckled face and letting Katy Belle bat playfully at her hair.

Sherri would laugh. "Yes, I guess she is."

Indeed, the kitten seemed to have two distinct moods: on and off. When she was on, she literally bounced off the walls, running through the house and up the wall, then back down and across the room again. She would hop onto the window screens and get her tiny claws stuck in the netting, and she would chase things that no one else in the Reed family could see. She played that way until she was exhausted, and then she would curl up in a fluffy gray heap on one of the girls' laps and sleep so soundly nothing could wake her.

Sarah and Samantha let the kitten sleep in their room, and most mornings they woke up to find her bouncing about their bedroom floor, running up the sides of their beds, and playfully pawing their faces.

"Oh, Katy Belle, I love you so much," Samantha would tell the kitten.

"Me, too, Katy Belle," Sarah would chime in.

The Reeds had begun attending a local Christian church in Cottonwood, Arizona, and each of them was excited about their new faith in God.

"Do you think God loves little Katy Belle as much as we do?" Samantha asked Sherri one afternoon.

Sherri pondered the question a moment and then smiled. "Well, he made Katy Belle. I suppose he loves her just like any of his creation."

The answer suited the young girl and she ran off to play. Later that week, Katy Belle got lost, and although the Reeds could hear her faint meow, they couldn't find her anywhere.

Finally, after they were about to give up, Sarah and Samantha's thirteen-year-old brother, Justin opened the refrigerator in search of a snack and there, sitting on the top shelf next to the milk, was Katy Belle.

"I found the kitten," Justin shouted. The rest of the family hurriedly joined him in the kitchen and stared in amazement as Katy Belle returned their gaze.

"Meow."

"How in the world did you get in the refrigerator?" Sherri laughed, sweeping the tiny cat from the shelf and holding her close. "Poor Katy Belle; you're freezing."

Sarah and Samantha took the kitten from their mother and spent an hour warming her up.

"Mom," Samantha said later, "I'm so glad she was okay. I don't know what I'd do if anything ever happened to Katy Belle. She's the best kitten we've ever had."

When school started in late August, the girls could hardly wait to run home from the bus stop and check on their kitten.

As August turned into September, the days grew even warmer and Sherri realized that the flea problem the animals had been fighting all summer was getting worse. She purchased more flea powder and a flea spray that promised to kill the insects immediately, and she gave the dog a treatment.

"There, girl, now you stay outside until those chemicals wear off," she told the dog when she finished. "The girls will be home soon and I don't want them breathing that stuff."

But during the next few days, Sherri noticed that she and her husband, Jeff, and the three kids were scratching at their ankles. One morning before school Sherri examined the small red welts along the girls' lower legs and sighed.

"Flea bites," she said. "That means they're in the house. Sarah, go get Katy Belle."

The pretty blond girl set off toward the bedroom and retrieved the kitten. "Why, Mom? She hasn't had fleas before, has she?"

Sherri shook her head. "No, but if they're in the house, then she's probably carrying them around, too."

Sherri did not have to search the kitten's silky fur for long to find several fleas working their way through her hair. "Yep, she's covered."

"What are we going to do?" Justin complained. "I can't keep getting bites on my legs, Mom. We have to do something."

"I know, son. Believe me, I don't like the bites any more than you do. I'll take care of the problem today while you kids are at school."

When the children had gone, Sherri examined the flea spray and found that it was safe to use on kittens. She sprayed Katy Belle thoroughly and then went about the house spraying the carpet and furniture. Hours later she felt she had finished the job and she vacuumed the house to remove any remaining fleas.

"That should do it," she muttered aloud. "Makes me wonder why I let animals stay in the house at all."

That evening, her house immaculate, Sherri noticed that her children were scratching less. *I guess I got 'em all,* she thought.

But the next morning, while Katy Belle was curled up on the sofa sleeping, Sherri decided to check her. There, on the kitten's warm underbelly, were three live fleas.

"Looks like you need another treatment, Katy Belle," Sherri said out loud, whisking the kitten into her arms and taking her outside onto the patio. She picked up the can of flea spray and gave the kitten another coating. Then she set her down on the carpet just inside the living room and went about her business.

Two hours later, she heard a soft sneezing sound and she began searching the house. The sound led her to the girls' bedroom, where she found Katy Belle, stretched out on Sarah's bed. Her eyes were swollen shut and runny and there was a gurgling sound each time she drew a breath.

"Oh, no, what's wrong with you?" Sherri said, stooping down to the kitten's level. When it was obvious that the kitten was struggling to breathe, she called her veterinarian.

She explained that the animals had brought fleas into the house and that she had used chemical cleaners on the carpet and furniture. She had sprayed the cat the day before and again that morning, she said. But she had done so according to the directions on the can.

The vet sighed. "Those aerosol flea sprays can be very, very bad for kittens," he said.

"But the can said as long as they're six weeks old it was fine."

"I know. Unfortunately, not all kittens can handle that kind of intense chemical treatment. You say you've sprayed her twice in twenty-four hours?"

"Yes. And she's been exposed to the carpet and the furniture. They have the chemicals, too."

The doctor listened again while Sherri described Katy Belle's condition.

"I'd tell you to bring her in, but it doesn't sound like there's much I can do."

"Meaning she'll get better on her own?"

"No," the vet replied. "I'm sorry, Sherri. I mean I don't think she's going to make it."

Sherri felt her heart sink. "So you're saying I've killed her?"

"It's not your fault. Those directions are much too liberal in my opinion. And no one wants fleas in their house. You did what anyone would have done in your situation."

"There's nothing I can do for her?"

"Why don't you give her a bath and see if that helps things."

Sherri hung up the phone and wondered what she would tell the girls when they got home. She walked slowly back to their bedroom and stroked Katy Belle with two fingers.

"Come on, Katy, girl, you can get through this," she whispered softly. In response the cat sneezed and then choked for several seconds.

Sherri closed her eyes and sighed. Then she picked up the kitten and carried her to the bathtub. She ran warm water and bathed the kitten, rinsing away the chemicals and hoping there would be some improvement.

Instead, the kitten grew much worse and thirty minutes after the bath she lay on her side, her body stiff, her mouth rigid and open. She was barely breathing and Sherri felt terrible. She tried to place a dropper of water in the kitten's mouth but it rolled back out and Sherri wondered how long it would be before she died.

When the girls got home that afternoon, they scampered back to their bedroom to play with Katy Belle. Instead, they found their mother huddled on the floor, her face very near the kitten's.

"What's wrong?" Sarah asked, stopping in her tracks.

Sherri looked up and the girls could see she'd been crying. "Katy Belle is having an allergic reaction to the flea spray."

Samantha moved closer and studied the kitten, seeing that she was lying stiff on her side, her breathing raspy. "How long before she gets over it?" Samantha asked.

Sherri studied her twins and sighed out loud. "Sit down, girls. I have something to tell you."

Sarah and Samantha did as they were told and sat cross-legged on the floor beside their mother.

"I called the vet and told him how Katy Belle was acting. She won't drink and she won't eat. She can barely breathe and she hasn't gotten any better since this morning."

"Let's take her in so the vet can fix her, Mom," Samantha said.

Sherri shook her head. "No. It isn't that easy this time, honey. The vet said that with a reaction like this, to this type of flea spray, kittens usually die. There's nothing he can do for her."

Sarah began crying and moved closer to Katy Belle, patting her gently on the top of her head. Samantha remained frozen in place.

"He said she would die?" Samantha asked.

"Probably. He said to watch her tonight and see if she gets better or worse. If she gets worse in the first twelve hours, then she'll die sometime tomorrow. I guess we just have to hope she gets better."

Samantha shook her head. "No, Mom, we don't have to hope about this. We have to pray about it. We've prayed about other things and God has answered us. Now we'll pray about Katy Belle. God loves us and he loves Katy Belle, so I know he'll hear us."

Sarah joined in. "That's right, Mom. Let's pray for Katy Belle. Then everything will be fine."

Sherri's mind raced, trying to think of a way to explain the situation to her young daughters. Yes, God would hear their prayers and yes he cared about them and their kitten. But nevertheless, the kitten was suffering from a fatal dose of chemical poisoning.

Help me, God, she prayed silently. *You have much more important things to take care of than this little kitten. But the girls' faith is so new. Show me what to do. I don't want them to lose faith over this.*

In that instant, she felt compelled to do the only thing that made sense. She took the hands of Samantha and Sarah, bowed her head, and closed her eyes.

"You girls go ahead," she said.

Samantha went first. "Dear God, we know you are real and that you love us," she prayed, her voice filled with sincerity. "Our little Katy Belle is very sick and she might die, God. Please make her better so she doesn't die."

When she was silent, Sarah took over. "Dear Lord, I love you so much and I know that you don't want Katy Belle to die. Please let her get better so she can run and play with us again."

When they finished the prayer, Samantha stood up and sat down on her bed next to the kitten.

"It's okay, Mom," she said. "You can go ahead. We'll watch over Katy Belle until she gets better."

Sherri looked at the struggling kitten and then back at her daughters. They were no longer on the verge of tears. Their faith that God would heal Katy Belle was absolute and now it was only a matter of loving her through the illness until her inevitable healing.

Sherri smiled at them and left the room, filled with doubts over what would happen next. She found a small cardboard box and placed a towel along the bottom. Then she took the kitten, placed her inside, and set the box in the garage.

"There aren't any chemicals out here so she'll probably be able to breathe better," she explained to the girls. "We'll keep a close eye on her, okay?"

The girls agreed and spent most of the afternoon and evening huddled together in the garage, cooing to Katy Belle and encouraging her to live. But after dinner, Katy Belle's body seemed even more stiff than before and her breathing was slow and labored.

When the girls went to bed that night, they prayed once more that God would heal their kitten. When they were asleep, Sherri checked on Katy Belle and tried once more to get her to drink.

She's barely alive, Sherri thought as she moved her fingers along the rigid kitten. Then Sherri closed her eyes and prayed. *Lord, please let me find her first. Then I can take care of her body and explain it to the girls later. If they wake up before me and find her dead, it'll be too much for them.*

By nine o'clock that evening, Katy Belle's entire body seemed to shudder as it struggled to draw each breath. Again Sherri felt frustrated by her inability to help the kitten. She telephoned the vet's home number, explained Katy Belle's symptoms and that the situation had grown more severe.

"Isn't there something that can be done for her?" she begged the vet.

"I'm sorry, not with this type of poisoning. She's dying, Sherri. It'll just be a matter of hours. If she's still suffering in the morning, you could bring her in and have her put to sleep if you'd like. It's up to you."

Sherri hung up the phone and thought of how disappointed the girls would be if their kitten was dead in the morning. She closed her eyes and breathed another prayer, trying to muster the faith she had heard in her daughters' voices earlier that evening.

Jeff was already in bed for the night and Sherri was tired. In that instant she knew that if there had been some way to put the kitten out of her misery there and then, she would have done it. She lifted the kitten's chin and felt tears well up in her eyes. "Good night, Katy Belle. You've been a good kitty."

Sherri turned and headed down the hallway for bed. Every hour that night she got up and checked on Katy Belle, hoping to be the first to find her when she died. But the kitten clung stubbornly to life.

The next morning, Sherri got up before the girls and tiptoed down the hall, through the kitchen, and into the garage in search of Katy Belle. She couldn't hear the raspy breathing and she wondered if the cat had already died. But when she peered into the box, she saw Katy Belle curled in a cozy ball and breathing almost normally.

"Katy Belle?"

She ran a finger under the kitten's chin and Katy Belle opened her eyes. She stared at Sherri and blinked twice. Then she settled back down and fell asleep once more.

"My God," she whispered, "you did work a miracle."

Just then Sarah and Samantha ran into the garage, their nightgowns flying behind them.

"Is she better, Mom?"

Sherri smiled and patted Katy Belle. "Yes, I think she's a little better."

The girls cheered and got down on their knees to pet the kitten, encouraging her to wake up. Finally, Katy Belle lifted her head once more and opened her eyes. They were still swollen and she struggled to adjust to the light. Then she stretched and stood up.

"Meow."

Sherri laughed in relief and cuddled the kitten close to her chest. "You're supposed to be dead, little girl," she said.

"What do you mean, she's supposed to be dead?" Samantha asked curiously.

"Well, honey, I told the vet how she was acting and how much flea spray I'd used. He said she wouldn't live another day."

"Yeah, but we asked God to heal her, remember?"

Sherri drew in a deep breath and smiled at the twins. "Yes, of course, but still she was supposed to be dead."

Sarah shook her head. "But that was before we prayed for her. When we take our problems to God, he takes care of them. Remember, Mom?"

Sherri laughed lightly, wondering at her two daughters, whose faith was so much simpler and stronger than her own.

"Actually," she said, pulling the girls close and staring in wonder at the kitten, who was once more snuggling into the towel and trying to sleep, "I think I'd forgotten. But thanks for reminding me."

In Memory of Chelsea

*D*r. Ken Culver first met Chelsea Ward in November 1985. Chelsea was eight months old, with twinkling eyes and a dimpled smile, and she found a place in the doctor's heart immediately.

At that point in his career, Dr. Culver had obtained his medical degree and was working in a specialty field—pediatric immunology—at Moffitt Hospital in San Francisco. The children he worked with all suffered from immune disorders, and Chelsea's illness was the most severe type of all.

The child suffered from ADA deficiency, a genetic condition wherein both parts of her immune system failed. The disease requires patients to live in a sterile, bubble-like environment, since almost any virus or bacteria can be life-threatening. Chelsea already suffered from a chronic lung infection and was in desperate need of help.

Doug and Jan Ward lived in Alberta, Canada, but

they knew their daughter's only chance for survival was to receive a bone marrow transplant—a procedure that was commonly performed at Moffitt Hospital. They wasted no time bringing her to San Francisco.

"We've rented an apartment and we're here as long as you can help her," Doug Ward told Dr. Culver when the two met.

Dr. Culver's heart went out to the young Wards, who were without family or friends in San Francisco. In the early weeks of their stay, the doctor and his wife, Cindy, befriended the couple and had them over for dinner on several occasions.

Doug was a top freestyle skier in Canada, and while he was in San Francisco, he and Dr. Culver would sometimes ride bikes together across the Golden Gate Bridge. They would pass the hours talking about the dreams each had followed and the high hopes they had for Chelsea's bone marrow transplant.

"We'll do the best we can for her, Doug," the doctor assured him.

"We love her so much," Doug said then, shaking his head and brushing back tears. "She's been sick most of her life but she's the happiest baby I've ever seen. I don't know what we'll do if . . ."

His voice trailed off and Dr. Culver understood. Chelsea had quickly found a special place in his heart and he had been praying for her survival since first meeting her. But despite his hopes, he knew the child's condition was gravely serious.

In the weeks leading up to the transplant, Chelsea was given high doses of chemotherapy and radiation to kill her diseased bone marrow. Dr. Culver watched the side effects take a terrible toll on the little girl.

Still, when he would dress in sterile garb and enter her room, she would grab her white security blanket and pull herself up to her feet. Braced against the side of the crib, she would grin at the doctor and babble in a sweet, singsong voice.

Finally, the day of the transplant arrived. Dr. Culver worked alongside Dr. Mort Cowan, retrieving several liters of bone marrow from Jan Ward's pelvis. The days immediately after the surgery would be the most dangerous, while they waited to see if Chelsea's body accepted or rejected her mother's marrow.

Please, Lord, help us, Dr. Culver prayed silently as he and the other doctor inserted a needle into Jan's pelvis and harvested her bone marrow. *Be with Chelsea now and help her small body accept this precious bone marrow.*

Dr. Culver's faith soared as they completed the retrieval process without a problem. After processing the marrow to remove cells that might be harmful to Chelsea's frail body, he carried the precious substance into the sealed room where Chelsea lay waiting. Surely the Lord had heard their prayers and the procedure would be a success.

Before administering the transplant, Dr. Culver, Doug, and Jan gathered around Chelsea's bed and prayed aloud.

"Thank you, God, for the success of today's bone marrow harvest and processing," the doctor said, his voice emotional. "Thank you for the gift of medicine and the difference it makes in our lives, and please help little Chelsea's body to accept the new bone marrow."

But not long after the transplant, Chelsea's chronic lung infection grew worse and the few antibodies she had in her system began attacking the new marrow.

Ten days after the transplant, Chelsea died.

Dr. Culver was overwhelmed with grief as he placed her lifeless body in the arms of her parents. He had suffered the loss of many young patients during his work with critically ill children. But Chelsea was different, special in a way he couldn't explain, and now she was gone.

Before the Wards left San Francisco, Dr. Culver spent an hour with Doug in his garage building the small casket that would carry Chelsea back to her home in Alberta. He stood beside Doug at the funeral home as Chelsea's white blanket was tucked in around her body and the casket lid was closed.

Dr. Culver returned to work, but the drive and purpose he'd known in the past was now confused; frustrated and disappointed.

He thought about the path that had led him into medicine and he remembered conversations he'd had with teachers and mentors along the way.

"You are a bright boy, Ken," one man had told him. "You will make a wonderful doctor."

"But I don't like blood."

"How do you know?"

"I don't know. But if I see a lot of it, I know I won't like it."

He had almost gone into teaching and coaching after that, but when he was alone, in prayer to God, he could not shake the feeling that the one thing he was supposed to do in life was be a doctor.

He remembered the time years earlier when he had worked with a terminally ill child named Gunther. The boy had a fatal kidney disorder. It was the first time one of Dr. Culver's patients had died, and the sight of a crying father and mother cradling their dead son in their arms had been life-changing.

"Here," the father had said. He handed Dr. Culver a toy that had hung on the side of Gunther's crib. "Give this to your baby boy. Please."

The Culver's first child, Ryan, was about the same age as Gunther, and the doctor took the toy gently from Gunther's grieving father. The toy was passed down to each of Dr. Culver's three children after that and acted as a symbol for the struggle and attachment involved in caring for terminally ill children.

Losing Gunther made Dr. Culver certain that he would not open a private practice and tend to children who were well. He would work with children who had devastating diseases, devoting himself to them and their families and praying he could someday make a difference.

But now that Chelsea had died, the certainty he had always felt about working with terminally ill children was gone. He wondered why God had not answered his prayers and helped Chelsea survive, and he finally concluded that Chelsea was happier, free of pain, in Heaven.

But still his spirits remained down, the memory of Chelsea's sweet smile fresh and painful in his mind.

"Why couldn't I save her, Lord?" he would ask during many sleepless nights that month. "Help me understand."

Then one day he received a letter from Chelsea's parents. Enclosed was an article from a Canadian newspaper speculating on the idea that gene therapy might help children like Chelsea.

Dr. Culver studied the article and considered the possibility. ADA deficiency was caused by the malfunction of the gene responsible for producing an enzyme critical for normal immune function. Experiments were already being conducted to see if there was a way to correct such a faulty gene.

Hope surged in the doctor for the first time since Chelsea's death. *Is this the way you want me to turn, God?* he wondered silently. *If conventional medicine is not helping children like Chelsea, would you have me work in research?*

The idea of moving his family to a city where research was being conducted, and giving up his daily interaction with patients, was depressing. But if this was the only way to help children like Chelsea, he would do it.

Show me if this is what you want, he prayed. *Give me a sign that you want me to conduct research and I'll go.*

A few months later, he was walking through the halls of Moffitt Hospital when another doctor stopped him. Through their conversation Dr. Culver learned of jobs at the National Institutes of Health (NIH) in Bethesda, Maryland, where he could study gene therapy.

Dr. Culver considered the thousands of genetic defects under investigation. Only one gene truly interested him—the one responsible for the disease that killed Chelsea. But he could be assigned to any of those under investigation if he took the job.

He discussed the dilemma with his church pastor and she shook her head. "Ken, I don't think it's the job for you. You're a people person."

Not long afterward, the family of a child he had cared for

invited him to dinner. Their daughter had recently died after fighting a severe genetic illness.

"Please don't leave," the girl's father said. "We need you here with the sick children."

Dr. Culver left their house that night not sure what to do. But in the end he went with his desire to find a better option for gravely ill children.

"I'll go to the interview, and if they offer me the job, I'll take it for three years," he told his wife, who was completely supportive of the idea. "A three-year commitment; that's it. If nothing comes of it, I'll get back to working with the kids. I just have a feeling this is something I'm supposed to do."

The interview went beautifully and within a few months the Culver family relocated in Bethesda. On Dr. Culver's first day at the research lab, the chief, Dr. Michael Blaese, approached him and explained that his assignment would be to work on ADA deficiency.

Dr. Culver was thrilled. It was the very condition that was responsible for Chelsea's death. This was the confirmation he had been looking for and he launched into his research with a renewed energy he hadn't known in the past year.

The next few years were financially difficult; in addition to working twelve-hour days at NIH, Dr. Culver took a second job working at a children's clinic. He built on the work of his colleagues, Dr. R. Michael Blaese and Dr. W. French Anderson, and tended to his experiments like a man driven to succeed.

Indeed, a framed picture of Chelsea sat on his new desk at the research center, and each day he remembered the sight of watching her parents tuck her white blanket around her body and close the lid of the homemade coffin.

Help me figure this out, Lord, he would pray. *So that my feeling of loss over Chelsea's death will make some sense.*

The experiments were looking more positive every week. Genes corrected in the laboratory were reintroduced into the blood of animals with surprising success. They were close to trying the procedure on a child, and Dr. Culver could hardly wait.

By then, another special little girl had entered Dr. Culver's life. Her name was Ashi DeSilva and she was a solemn child with huge brown eyes and pretty dark hair.

Dr. Culver worked with samples of the sick child's blood and watched incredulously. When he supplied the white blood cells with a laboratory-produced normal gene, Ashi's cells began producing healthy ADA.

Finally, on September 14, 1990, Dr. Culver stood over a cell culture and prayed. The culture contained Ashi's blood cells infused with the ADA gene Dr. Culver and others had designed in the lab.

After decades of consideration by the medical community and years of painstaking experimentation, Dr. Culver was about to perform the first transfusion of genetically designed cells. The procedure was of worldwide importance and the media awaited word on its outcome.

Ashi, who had just turned four, had been transferred to NIH and waited in the intensive care unit. Dr. Culver stared once more at the unremarkable yellowish liquid before him and placed it in a plastic bag.

"Here goes," he said aloud as he headed for the tenth floor, where Ashi waited. "Please let it work, Lord."

He opened the door to Ashi's room and found her watching *Sesame Street*. Her parents stood by the bed as Dr. Culver connected a small dose to the intravenous needle attached to Ashi's hand. He would try this amount initially, in order to check for adverse reactions. If there were none, he would supply her with the entire contents of the bag.

This is in your memory, Chelsea, he thought. Then he started the infusion.

There was a heavy moment of anticipation as Dr. Culver monitored the child's vital signs. But they remained unchanged, and in minutes the first human gene therapy was in progress.

Dr. Culver watched, his eyes watery from the emotion of the moment. The therapy was limited to a single genetic defect and would not offer a permanent cure. Ashi would have to return for periodic infusions until more progress could be made in the genetic research. But it could also mean the difference between life and death, the difference between a sterile environment and that of any other child. It was a monumental step.

Weeks passed and Ashi took to the therapy beautifully. Other than her weekly medicine and occasional visits to the research center for infusions, she was able to live a completely normal life. The success gained Drs. Culver, Blaese, and Anderson worldwide attention, and the procedure has been used to treat numerous children since then.

Over the years that followed, Ashi would send Dr. Culver notes and drawings, and once in a while, when she visited the center for an infusion, she would bring a report card.

"Look, Doctor," she would say, beaming, her face not nearly so solemn as before. "Teacher says I'm one of the best in class."

Those times Dr. Culver was absolutely certain he had done the right thing and that God had shown him the unexpected miracle not only of Chelsea's life, but also of her death. He would study Ashi's smiling eyes and see, within them, the eyes of Chelsea.

Somewhere, he thought, *Chelsea is smiling, too.*

But in case he ever wonders about the importance of his research, he has only to glance atop his desk and look into the twinkling eyes of the child he will never forget, a little girl with smiling dimples, clutching a soft, white blanket. Then he will be driven for yet another day, making further progress in the field of genetic research, working in part for the memory of Chelsea Ward.